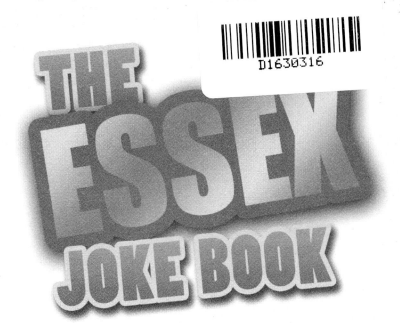

THE ESSEX JOKE BOOK

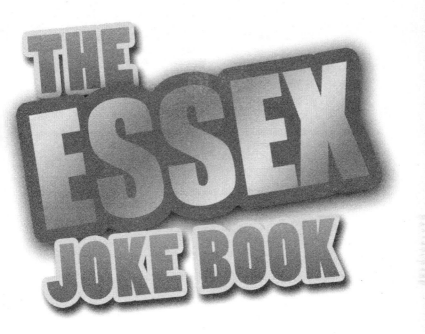

# THE ESSEX JOKE BOOK

## NICHOLAS KNIGHTS

### ILLUSTRATED BY ANDREW PINDER

Virgin BOOKS

2 4 6 8 10 9 7 5 3 1

First published in Great Britain in 2012 by Virgin Books,
an imprint of Ebury Publishing
A Random House Group Company

Illustrations by Andrew Pinder

www.randomhouse.co.uk

Addresses for companies within The Random House Group Limited can be
found at www.randomhouse.co.uk/offices.htm

The Random House Group Limited Reg. No. 954009

A CIP catalogue record for this book is available from the British Library

The Random House Group Limited supports The Forest Stewardship
Council (FSC®), the leading international forest certification organisation.
Our books carrying the FSC label are printed on FSC® certified paper.
FSC is the only forest certification scheme endorsed by the leading environmental
organisations, including Greenpeace. Our paper procurement policy can be
found at www.randomhouse.co.uk/environment

Designed by K DESIGN, Somerset

Typeset in Helvetica Neue by Palimpsest Book Production Limited,
Falkirk, Stirlingshire

Printed and bound by CPI Group (UK) Ltd, Croydon, CR0 4YY

ISBN: 9780753541081

# CONTENTS

Some of these jokes are a bit raunchy, innit.
Well, whaddya expect from *The Essex Joke
Book*? Enjoy!

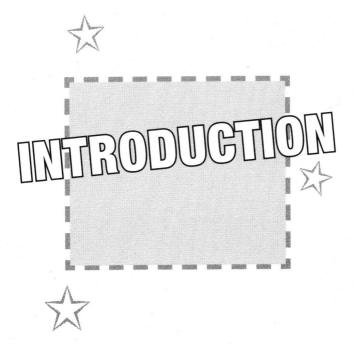

INTRODUCTION

Once a Roman stronghold, Essex is now home to a breed of people that would have had Pliny the Elder scratching his head for suitable adjectives. The girls, with their fake tans, fake hair and fake boobs, are depicted as being so dim they must have sneaked into the gene pool when the lifeguard wasn't looking. They have tight clothes and loose morals. Meanwhile the boys are portrayed as being flash chancers who have more bravado than brains and spend almost as much time on their appearance as the girls.

Of course, these are stereotypes and down the years there have been many notable exceptions to the rule. Dame Maggie Smith was born in Essex (Ilford), as was Dudley Moore (Dagenham) and

*Countdown* brainbox Rachel Riley (Rochford). Even U2's The Edge was born in Barking. Mind you, his family moved to Ireland when he was one, so he's not a proper Essex Boy. And let's face it, no self-respecting Essex Boy would hide his immaculately coiffed hair under a woolly hat for thirty years. International rock star or not, he wouldn't have pulled a bird at Decadence in Chelmsford dressed like that.

Some Essex folk may be offended by the jokes in this book. But they are not meant to be faithful representations of the lives Essex people lead, as I was explaining to my dear eighty-six-year-old granny from Basildon shortly before she went off for a vajazzle.

Nicholas Knights

# ESSEX GIRLS

*What's the first thing an Essex Girl does*
*when she wakes up in the morning?*
She goes home.

On her first trip to Spain, an Essex Girl visits Marbella. She wants to check out the local nightclub and so she asks a police officer for directions.

'Wait here at the bus stop for bus number 88,' he says. 'It'll take you right there.'

Four hours later, he sees her still waiting at the bus stop. 'I said to wait for bus number 88. That was four hours ago. Why are you still here?'

'Don't worry,' says the Essex Girl. 'It won't be long now. The eighty-third bus just went by.'

*What can strike an Essex Girl without her even knowing it?*
A thought.

*How do you spot an Essex Girl at a funeral?*
She's the one who catches the wreath.

Desperate for money, an Essex Girl decides to kidnap a child and demand a ransom. So she goes to a playground, takes a small boy behind some bushes and tells him: 'I've kidnapped you.' She then writes a note to his parents saying: 'I've kidnapped your son. Put £100,000 in a bag and place it under the slide in the playground tomorrow at 2 p.m. Signed, Essex Girl.' She pins the note to the boy's shirt, tells him to show it to his parents and sends him home.

The next day, just after 2 p.m., the Essex Girl spots a bag under the slide as expected. She opens the bag and finds £100,000 and a note that says: 'How could you do this to a fellow Essex Girl?'

An Essex Girl goes into a café and sees a waitress with a name tag on her shirt. 'Lovely!' the Essex Girl gushes. 'What did you name the other one?'

*What's an Essex Girl's favourite wine?*
'I wanna go to Lakeside!'

*Why does an Essex Girl wear knickers?*
To keep her ankles warm.

An Essex Girl goes to the doctor's and complains about a sore throat. The doctor sits her down, gets out his flashlight and says: 'Open wide.'

'I can't,' replies the Essex Girl. 'The arms on this chair get in my way.'

An Essex Girl goes into Pizza Hut and orders a pizza.

'Do you want it cut into six pieces or twelve?' asks the waitress.

'Six, please,' says the Essex Girl. 'I don't think I could eat twelve.'

*How is an Essex Girl like a restaurant?*
She only takes deliveries in the rear.

*How is an Essex Girl like a £10 note?*
She gets passed from man to man.

*Did you hear about the Essex Girl who thought 'love handles' referred to her ears?*

*Why did the Essex Girl climb on the roof?*
She heard drinks were on the house.

*Why don't Essex Girls like pickled gherkins?*
They keep getting their head stuck in the jar.

*How do you amuse an Essex Girl for hours?*
Write 'PTO' on both sides of a piece of paper.

*What do a bowling ball and an Essex Girl
have in common?*
They'll probably both end up in the gutter.

A ventriloquist is performing at the Palace Theatre, Southend. Tailoring his act to a local audience, he trots out a selection of Essex Girl jokes, which greatly offends a young woman in the third row. Halfway through his act, she stands up and yells: 'OK, mate, I've heard enough of your denigrating Essex Girl jokes. What makes you think you can stereotype us in that way? How is someone's county of birth relevant to her worth as a human being? It's blokes like you who prevent women like me from being respected and from realising my full potential in the workplace. It may just be comic banter to you, but to us it's insulting and demeaning to portray all girls from Essex as nothing more than dim bimbos.'

Flustered, the ventriloquist begins to apologise, but the young woman interrupts him angrily. 'You stay out of this, mister,' she shouts. 'I'm talking to that little f**ker on your knee!'

*What did the Essex Girl do when she missed
the number 86 bus?*
She caught the number 43 twice.

*Why did the Essex Girl keep running around
the bed?*
She was trying to catch up with her sleep.

*How many Essex Girls does it take to change
a light bulb?*
Two. One to hold the Bacardi Breezer and
one to yell 'Daddy!'

As part of her college textile course, Chardonnay
decides to knit her young nephew some socks.
Then she receives a letter from the boy's mother
saying he has grown another foot since she
last saw him. So Chardonnay starts knitting a
third sock.

*Why wasn't the Virgin Mary an Essex Girl?*
She wouldn't have been old enough
to bear children.

*How do you get an Essex Girl out of a tree?*
*Wave.*

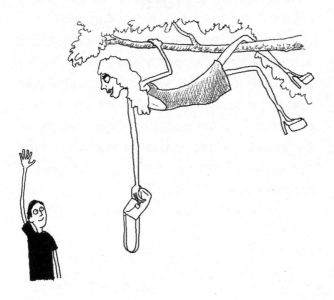

A little boy is crying in a Romford supermarket. A man asks him what the matter is.

'I can't find Mummy,' the boy replies.

'What's Mummy like?' asks the man.

The child replies: 'Holidays in Ibiza and Bacardi Breezers.'

A visitor to London goes into a bar and after several drinks he announces loudly: 'Does anyone want to hear an Essex Girl joke?'

A deathly hush falls over the place until the barmaid informs him in menacing tones: 'I think you ought to know, mister, that I'm an Essex Girl, my boss is an Essex Girl, my assistant is an Essex Girl, the woman on that stool is an Essex Girl, and the woman at that table in the corner is an Essex Girl. So do you still want to tell that Essex Girl joke?'

'No,' he says. 'Not if I've got to explain it five times!'

*Did you hear about the wannabe Essex dancer who thought a* pas de deux *was a father of twins?*

An Essex Girl walks into a library and says: 'Can I have a burger and fries, please?'

'I'm sorry,' says the librarian, 'but this is a library.'

So the Essex Girl whispers: 'Can I have a burger and fries, please?'

An Essex Girl goes to the police station to report that she has been assaulted.

'When did this happen?' asks the desk sergeant.
'Eight days ago.'
'Why did you wait until now to report it?'
'Well,' says the Essex Girl, 'I didn't know I had been assaulted till his bloody cheque bounced.'

*How does an Essex Girl know when she's been sleepwalking?*
She wakes up in her own bed.

An Essex Girl is walking down the street with her designer blouse wide open. A police officer stops her and says: 'Excuse me, Miss, do you know your blouse is open?'

'OMG!' shrieks the Essex Girl. 'I've left my baby on the bus!'

*Why did the Essex Girl water only half of her window box?*
She'd heard there was a fifty per cent chance of rain.

*What did the Essex Girl's mum say to her before her date?*
'If you're not in bed by eleven, come home.'

A Scouser meets an Essex Girl in a club. He asks her where in Essex she lives.

She replies: 'Walton.'

'That's funny,' he says. 'There's a place in Liverpool that shares the same name.'

'Really?' she says. 'What's it called?'

After a night out in London, Sharon is travelling home on the Central Line to catch the last train from Liverpool Street when she reads a sign saying: 'Dogs must be carried on the escalator.'

'OMG!' she thinks. 'Where am I going to find a dog at this time of night?'

An Essex Girl is summoned to appear as a witness in a court case. The prosecutor asks her: 'Where were you on the night of July 12th?'

'Your honour,' says the defence lawyer, interrupting, 'the whereabouts of the witness on the night of July 12th has no bearing on the case.'

'It's OK,' says the Essex Girl from the witness box. 'I don't mind answering the question.'

'No, I object,' repeats the defence lawyer.

'Honestly,' insists the Essex Girl, 'it's not a problem. I'll answer.'

The judge rules: 'If the witness insists on answering, there is no reason for the defence to object.'

'I request an adjournment,' says the defence lawyer.

'Very well,' says the judge wearily. 'The court will adjourn for twenty minutes while I sort this matter out with the two lawyers.'

Twenty minutes later, the court reconvenes, and the judge begins: 'As I ruled earlier, if the witness is happy to answer the question, the defence has no right to object in law. So the prosecution may ask the question.'

'Thank you, your honour,' says the prosecutor. Turning to the witness stand, he asks once more: 'Where were you on the night of July 12th?'

The Essex Girl replies brightly: 'I don't remember.'

*How many Essex Girls does it take to make a circuit?*
Two. One to stand in the bath, and another to pass her the hairdryer.

---

An Essex Girl is standing at a vending machine in a casino. She inserts a pound coin, pushes the button and catches the bar of chocolate when it comes out. After she repeats the process a dozen more times, the casino manager comes over to her and says: 'You must be really hungry.'

'Not really,' she says. 'I just don't want to stop while I'm winning.'

*Why were there bullet holes in the mirror?*
An Essex Girl had tried to shoot herself.

*Why don't Essex Girls vote?*
They can't spell X.

An Essex Girl goes to the doctor complaining of morning sickness. 'Congratulations!' says the doctor. 'Do you know who the father is?'

The Essex Girl replies: 'If you ate a tin of baked beans, would you know which one made you fart?'

*Why did the Essex Girl have sex in the microwave?*
Because she wanted to have a baby in nine minutes.

A girl goes to the doctor's in Ipswich.

Touching every part of her body with her finger, she tells the doctor: 'It hurts everywhere. My arm hurts, my leg hurts, my head hurts, my neck hurts, my shoulder hurts. What do you think the problem is, Doctor?'

The doctor briefly examines her and says: 'Are you originally from Essex by any chance?'

'Yes, I lived in Brentwood till last year,' she gushes. 'Why?'

The doctor replies: 'Because the problem is you have a broken finger.'

*Did you hear about the Essex Girl who got locked in the bathroom?*
She was in there so long, she peed her pants.

*What's the difference between an Essex Girl and the Panama Canal?*
One's a busy ditch . . .

*Why can't Essex Girls water ski?*
Because their legs spread as soon as their
crotch gets wet.

An Essex Girl goes to the local hospital to donate
blood. 'What type are you?' asks the nurse.
The Essex Girl replies: 'I'm an outgoing cat-lover.'

*What's the irritating part around an Essex
Girl's vagina?*
The Essex Girl.

*What's an Essex Girl's favourite nursery
rhyme?*
Humpme Dumpme.

An Essex Girl goes to the doctor and says: 'It's
been a month since my last visit, but I'm not
feeling any better.'

'OK,' says the doctor, 'did you follow the
instructions on the medicine I gave you?'

'Yes I did,' replies the Essex Girl. 'The bottle
said: "Keep tightly closed."'

An Essex Girl arrives home to find that her house
has been burgled. Worried in case the burglar is still
on the premises, she immediately calls the police

who send the nearest patrol in the area, which happens to be a dog handler.

Seeing the policeman and his dog approach the house, the Essex Girl suddenly bursts into tears.

'What's the matter?' asks the policeman.

'You're 'avin' a laugh, in't yer? I come home to find all my possessions stolen, so I call the police for help, and what do they do? They send me a blind policeman!'

*How did the Essex Girl break her leg raking*
*leaves?*
She fell out of the tree.

*Why did the Essex Girl fall out of the window?*
She was ironing the curtains.

An Essex Girl sees a sign which says 'Press bell for night watchman'. So she presses the bell, and soon she hears the night watchman plodding down the stairs. Slowly he produces a bunch of keys from his pocket and proceeds to unlock first one iron gate, then another. Finally, after disabling the alarm system, he unlocks a third gate and says: 'Well, what do you want?'

The Essex Girl replies: 'I just wanted to know why you can't ring the bell yourself.'

On holiday in Spain, a young woman goes to the local doctor and complains of feeling unwell. 'I think I might have some sort of virus,' she says.

'I see you are from Essex,' says the Spanish doctor. 'In that case, to be on the safe side, stay out of bed for two days.'

The phone rings in Maxine's Brentwood flat at three o'clock in the morning.

'Is that the Pink Hippo?' asks the voice on the other end.

'No,' says Maxine, 'this is a private residence.'

'I must have the wrong number,' says the caller. 'Sorry to trouble you at this time of night.'

'Oh, that's OK,' says Maxine. 'I had to get up anyway to answer the phone.'

---

Mandy from Essex is spending the weekend with friends in Norfolk. On the Sunday morning, after a heavy night of Lambrinis, she slips a bottle of Evian into her Louis Vuitton and goes for a short walk in the country. Soon she comes across a farmer guiding his sheep across the lane.

'OMG!' she shrieks. 'I've never seen so many sheep. They're so cute . . . and, er, sheepy. Mr Farmer, if I can guess how many sheep you've got, can I take one home with me?'

'I suppose so,' says the farmer, a sucker for a pretty face.

Mandy closes her eyes in concentration and says: 'OMG, my brain hurts! Just think of a number, Mand. Think of a number. 286.'

'That's right!' says the farmer, amazed. 'OK, which sheep do you want?'

Mandy picks the cutest animal and beams contentedly.

'Right,' says the farmer, 'now I've got a challenge for you. If I can guess which county you're from, can I have my dog back?'

---

*Why did the Essex Girl throw bread into the toilet?*
She wanted to feed the toilet duck.

*How do you confuse an Essex Girl?*
Put her in a round room and tell her to sit in the corner.

Despite being used to travelling by train, Aimee had never flown before. Boarding her first flight at Stansted, she asks the stewardess: 'Excuse me, does all of the plane go to Marbella or is it just the front part?'

*Why did the Essex Girl decide not to go water skiing?*
She couldn't find a lake with a slope.

For her twenty-fifth birthday, Lauren from Dagenham went on her first parachute jump. There were six other novices making their first jumps that day and before going up in the plane, the instructor patiently went through all the safety procedures. He told them that they would need to start preparing for landing when they were at 300 feet.

Lauren put her hand up and asked: 'How am I supposed to know when I'm at 300 feet?'

'That's a good question,' said the instructor. 'When you get to 300 feet, you can recognise the faces of people on the ground.'

After thinking about his answer for a moment, Lauren asked: 'What happens if there is no one there I know?'

An embarrassed silence fell on the room.

An Essex Girl walks into a bar holding a lump of dog poo. 'How lucky am I!' she tells the barman. 'I very nearly stepped in this!'

*How did the Essex Girl die drinking milk?*
The cow fell on her.

*What's the similarity between an Essex Girl and a cow pat?*
The older they get, the easier they are to pick up.

*What's the difference between an Essex Girl and an ironing board?*
It's not always easy to get an ironing board's legs open.

*What's the difference between an Essex Girl and the Grand Old Duke of York?*
The Grand Old Duke of York only had 10,000 men.

An Essex Girl and an Irishman are sitting at a bar when she notices something strange about the wellies he is wearing. "'Scuse me, mate,' she says. 'I ain't bein' funny or nuffink, but why does one of your wellies have an L on it and the other one's got an R on it?'

The Irishman puts down his pint of Guinness and smiles. 'It's to help me remember which boot goes on which foot. The one with L goes on the left foot and the R goes on the right foot.'

'Oh, I geddit,' says the Essex Girl. 'That must be why my knickers have C and A on them.'

*What's the difference between an Essex Girl and a brick?*
When you lay a brick, it doesn't follow you around afterwards.

*How can you tell if an Essex Girl is having a bad day?*
Her tampon is behind her ear and she can't find her pencil.

ESSEX
BOYS

An Essex Boy comes in from the kitchen with a puzzled look on his face.

'I don't know what's happened,' he tells his mother. 'I was rinsing some ice cubes a few minutes ago and now I can't find them!'

*Why doesn't Viagra work on Essex Boys?*
Because they only get hard when they've got their mates with them.

*How do you sink a submarine full of Essex Boys?*
Knock on the door.

Dave says to Kev: 'I've been getting a bit too close to my ex lately.'

'Yeah?'

'Yeah. Bloody restraining order!'

*Why did the Essex Boy put ice in his condom?*
To keep the swelling down.

---

Mark walks into a Brentwood bar to be greeted by his mates. The banter starts immediately.

'Oi, Mark,' they laugh. 'You put on a great show with your missus last night. You left the light on in your bedroom and we could see everything that was going on projected on to your curtains. We had no idea she was so up for it!'

'Sorry to spoil your fun, lads,' says Mark, 'but the joke's on you. I wasn't at home last night.'

---

*Why did the Essex photographer ask for some burned-out light bulbs?*
He needed them for his darkroom.

*What do you call an Essex Boy in a black leather jacket?*
A rebel without a clue.

Ricky is so proud of his new pair of shoes that he decides to wear them on Friday to a Romford nightclub. After dancing with one girl for a few minutes, he says: 'Listen, I bet I can guess the colour of your knickers.'

'OK,' she grins. 'What colour do you think they are?'

'Pink,' he replies.

'How did you know that?' she asks incredulously.

'I saw the reflection in my shiny new shoes.'

'Here,' she says, 'dance with my sister and see if you can work out what colour knickers she has on.'

After dancing with her sister for a while, Ricky starts rubbing the toes of his shoes on the legs of his trousers. Then he dances again. But a few minutes later, he concedes defeat. 'I give up,' he says. 'What colour knickers have you got on? I just can't seem to make them out.'

She giggles: 'I'm not wearing knickers.'

'Thank God for that!' says Ricky. 'I thought for a moment I had a crack in my new shoes.'

---

An Essex Girl gives birth to twins. Her Essex Boy husband is furious and demands to know who the father of the other baby is.

---

*Did you know that violent crime and obesity are now so common in Essex that many Essex Boys are afraid to go out, in case they are attacked by teenagers with a knife . . . and a fork?*

Joey had a thing about older women, and one night in a Southend club a mature lady caught his eye. While his mates were chatting up the brash local girls, Joey was drawn to the woman sitting alone with an empty glass in a dark corner. He reckoned she was probably in her early fifties but could easily pass for ten years younger. She had immaculate shoulder-length auburn hair and was wearing a cream top and a knee-length chocolate-brown leather skirt. To Joey she oozed class and sex, but not necessarily in that order.

With the confidence of youth, he sauntered over and asked if he could buy her a drink. She readily accepted and they started chatting. Very quickly the chatting turned to flirting. While his mates were getting knocked back one by one, Joey had the feeling that this was going to be a night to remember.

Within half an hour of meeting, they were kissing passionately. It was at this point that she whispered in his ear: 'Have you ever had a mother and daughter together?'

Joey could hardly believe his luck. 'No,' he spluttered, 'but it's something I've always fantasised about.'

'Well, tonight could be the night your dreams come true,' she purred, finishing off another double vodka. With that, she took him by the hand and led him from the club. His mates could only watch in astonishment.

'It's only a five-minute walk to my place,' she said. He could barely contain himself at the thought of bedding mother and daughter together, his ultimate fantasy threesome. Wait till he told his mates the next day!

After what seemed an eternity given his state of anticipation and arousal, they reached her house. She gave him a knowing look, turned the key in the front door, put the hall light on and shouted upstairs: 'Are you still awake, Mother?'

A Geordie, an Irishman and an Essex Boy are drinking together in a Benidorm bar. The Geordie says: 'This is a good bar but where I come from in Newcastle there's an even better place – Robson's. You buy a drink, you buy another drink, and then Robson himself buys you a third drink.'

The others agree it sounds a great bar, but then the Irishman says: 'In Dublin there's a bar called O'Malley's. You buy a drink, O'Malley buys you a drink, you buy another drink, and O'Malley buys you another drink.'

The others agree that it sounds a fantastic bar, but then the Essex Boy says: 'Where I come from in Billericay there's a bar called Dave's. Dave buys you your first drink, your second drink and your third drink. Then he fixes you up with a date and guarantees you'll get laid.'

'Wow!' say the others. 'That's brilliant. Did that actually happen to you?'

'No,' says the Essex Boy, 'but it happened to my sister.'

A graffiti artist spray-painted GNAB on the side of a Brentwood church. Mick saw it and said to his mate Harry: 'That's bang out of order!'

Inspired by gangster films, a gang of Essex Boys decide to rob a bank. For three months they painstakingly dig a tunnel from beneath a neighbouring shop to emerge in the heart of the bank's vault.

On the night of the raid, the gang emerge from the tunnel and set to work. They are expecting one or two safes filled with cash and valuables, but are pleased to find instead hundreds of smaller safes. 'This is our lucky day!' smiles the gang leader.

However, when they open the first safe, the robbers find only a small pot of vanilla pudding. 'No sweat,' they think. 'At least there's something for us to eat while we open all the other safes.'

The second safe also contains nothing but a pot of vanilla pudding, and it proves the same with every other safe in the building. No cash, no gold, no jewels, just countless pots of vanilla pudding. After three hours of opening safes, the dejected robbers exit via the tunnel, leaving with nothing more than queasy, full stomachs.

The following day's headline in the *Evening Standard* reads 'London's Largest Sperm Bank Robbed'.

Dave is meeting Kev in a bar, and as he walks in he notices two pretty girls looking at him. He hears one girl say to the other: 'Nine.'

Pleased with himself, he swaggers over to Kev at the bar and tells him that the blonde in the corner has just rated him a nine out of ten.

'Sorry to disappoint you, mate,' says Kev, 'but when I walked in, those two girls were speaking German!'

*Why did the Essex Boy buy his girlfriend
fishnet stockings?*
She told him she had crabs.

*What do you call the skeleton of an Essex
Boy in a wardrobe?*
Last year's hide-and-seek champion.

*Did you hear about the Essex Boy who
thought the world's most prolific inventor was
an Irishman named Pat Pending?*

Lee is boasting about his glamorous new girlfriend.

'You're 'aving a laugh, in't yer?' says Mikey. 'That bird's been with every bloke in Billericay!'

Lee thinks about this for a second before replying: 'Billericay isn't *such* a big town.'

---

A group of Essex Boys are walking along the road when they come to a high brick wall. Wondering what is behind the wall, three of them give the fourth a leg-up so that he can peer over the top.

'It looks like one of them nudist camps,' he reports.

'Men or women?' ask the others.

'I dunno,' he says. 'They ain't got no clothes on.'

---

Jim and Billy find three hand grenades and decide that they ought to take them to Romford police station.

'What if one of them explodes before we get there?' asks Jim.

'Don't worry,' says Billy. 'We'll just lie and tell them we only found two.'

An Essex Boy is walking down Brentwood High Street when he sees a girl with enormous breasts.

"'Scuse me, darlin',' he says, 'I just want to say you've got the most amazing boobs I've ever seen.'

'Thank you,' she says. 'I had 'em done last year, didn't I?'

'Listen,' he continues, 'I don't know whether you're up for this, but I would pay you £500 if you'd just let me bite them.'

'What are you, some kind of pervert?' she rages, and starts to storm off, but he races after her and grabs her by the arm.

'No, no,' he protests. 'I'm just in love with your boobs. They are truly amazing creations. I tell you what, I'll pay you £1,000 if you'll let me bite them. Don't worry, I'll be really gentle.'

Momentarily tempted, she starts to think of all the make-up and tanning sessions she could buy for £1,000, but quickly comes to her senses. 'No way,' she says. 'Get lost.'

'OK,' he says, '£5,000 just to let me bite them. That's my final offer. We'll go somewhere discreet. No one will ever know.'

She is seriously wavering now. 'You'd pay me £5,000 just to bite my boobs? And you promise not to tell anyone?'

'I promise.'

'OK then, it's a deal. There's an alley just round the corner where no one will see us.'

So they disappear into the quiet alley and she lifts up her top and undoes her bra. He then starts to fondle, caress and squeeze her mighty breasts.

'Hurry up then,' she says impatiently. 'Are you gonna bite them or what?'

'No,' he says. 'Too expensive.'

*Why did the Essex Boy cross the road?*
To happy slap the chicken.

An Essex Boy arrives home and tells his girl-friend that he's been banned from the local B&Q.

'Why?' she asks. 'What happened?'

'Well,' he says, 'this bloke in overalls came up to me and asked if I wanted decking, so I thought I'd get the first punch in.'

Mark asks Reg: 'Do you talk to your girlfriend while you're having sex?'

'Only if she phones,' says Reg.

*Why do Essex Boys wear hoodies?*
To hide the gap where their brain should be.

*How do you know if an Essex Boy is a bad father?*
He lets his thirteen-year-old daughter smoke in front of her kids.

Dave and Kev are viewing a girl's profile on a dating website: Blonde 23 From London Great Personality 5ft 3 Green Eyes. Dave sighs: 'Don't get me wrong, I like short birds. But three green eyes? No wonder she can't find a bloke!'

Two Essex Boys go off on a long fishing weekend to the Norfolk Broads. They hire a smart lakeside cabin and all the equipment, but at the end of their three-day break they have only managed to catch one fish.

As they are driving home, one turns to the other and says: 'Don't get me wrong, I've had a great time, but do you realise that this one measly fish has cost us £600?'

'Blimey!' says his friend. 'It's a good job we didn't catch any more then!'

Bob says to Danny: 'I'll never forget that terrifying moment I saw my first grey pubic hair.'
'Yeah?'
'Yeah. It was on a kebab.'

An Essex Boy buys an electric car, but the next day he phones the dealership to complain. 'That new electric car you sold me yesterday will only go ten yards,' he says.

The salesman is puzzled. 'Is the battery charged up?' he asks.

'Yes.'

'Is the brake off?'

'Yes.'

'Is it in gear?'

'Yes.'

'Well, I don't understand it. What makes you think the car will only go ten yards?'

'Because,' says the Essex Boy, 'that's as far as the lead will stretch from the socket.'

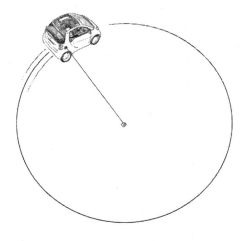

Reg and Mick are eyeing up two girls in a nightclub.

'What d'you reckon to that bird over there, the one in the blue top?' asks Reg.

'Nah,' says Mick. 'She's an aeroplane blonde.'

'A what?'

'An aeroplane blonde. Still got a black box.'

Two Essex Boys in a lorry are approaching a low bridge. The clearance says 10 foot 6 inches but when they stop, get out and measure the lorry, they find that it is 11 foot high.

One turns to the other and says: 'Listen, I can't see any police around. Let's go for it.'

# BRAINBOXES AND BIMBOS

*What's the difference between*
*Essex and Mars?*
There might be intelligent life on Mars.

*What do you get if you offer an Essex Girl*
*a penny for her thoughts?*
Change.

*How do you change an Essex Girl's mind?*
Blow in her ear.

*What do you call six Essex Girls in a row?*
A wind tunnel.

*What do you call an Essex Girl with
two brain cells?*
Pregnant.

Kelly is browsing the shelves at Billericay Library one day when a book title catches her eye. It's called *How to Hug* and she thinks it will suit her caring, sharing personality.

So she takes it to the desk, but the librarian tells her: 'I'm sorry, you can't take that book out. It's reference only.'

'What do you mean?' says Kelly in disbelief. 'How can a book called *How to Hug* be reference only? It's for everyone!'

'*How to Hug* is not the title,' explains the librarian patiently. 'It's volume seven of *Encyclopedia Britannica*.'

*Why did the Essex Girl climb over
the glass wall?*
To see what was on the other side.

*What do you see when you peer into an
Essex Girl's eyes?*
The back of her head.

*How do you make an Essex Girl's*
*eyes sparkle?*
Shine a torch into her ear.

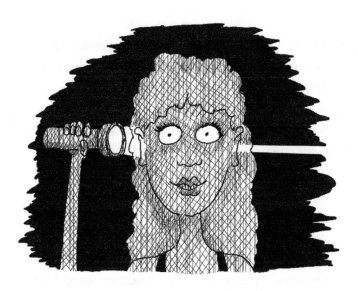

A maths teacher at a Harlow school asks one
of his teenage girl pupils: 'How many degrees
are there in a circle?'
'This is a trick question,' she answers. 'Do you
want Fahrenheit or Celsius?'

*Why did the Essex Boy stare at the carton of orange juice?*
Because it said 'concentrate'.

As the wine flowed at an Essex dinner party, the four guests started discussing who they thought was the greatest genius in history.

One man said: 'For me it has to be Mozart. Anyone who can create such great music at such a young age has to be a genius.'

His wife said: 'What about Shakespeare? To write so many fantastic plays makes him a real genius.'

'Very true,' said the other husband, 'but I reckon the greatest genius of all time was Einstein. Anyone who can master maths is a genius in my book.' Turning to his wife, he continued: 'What do you think, Shell?'

'The people you've mentioned were all very good,' she said, 'but to my mind the man who invented the clock was the greatest genius. I mean, how did he know what time it was?'

*What do you call an intelligent woman in Essex?*
A tourist.

Leanne decides to broaden her horizons and inject a spot of culture into her life by going to the theatre in Basildon. The next day, she bumps into a friend in the street who asks how she enjoyed her first-ever play.

'I saw the first act,' says Leanne, 'but not the second.'

'Why didn't you stay?' asks the friend.

'Cos it said on the programme "Act Two: Five years later" and I couldn't wait that long.'

*How do you make an Essex Girl laugh on a Friday?*
Tell her a joke on a Monday.

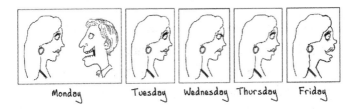

Monday    Tuesday    Wednesday    Thursday    Friday

An Essex Girl is walking down the street when a car pulls up and the driver asks: 'Is there a B&Q in Chelmsford?'

'Don't ask me,' says the Essex Girl. 'I can't spell to save my life!'

*What's the first question on an*
*Essex quiz night?*
Wot you lookin' at?

An Essex Girl playing Trivial Pursuit at a board-game night lands on a Science and Nature question. The question is: 'If you are in a vacuum and someone calls your name, can you hear it?'

After a moment's thought, she asks: 'Is the vacuum on or off?'

*What did the Essex Boy say when his aunt*
*bought him a book for his birthday?*
'Fanks, but I've got one already.'

An Essex Girl goes into a shop and asks the man behind the counter what the time is.

'2.35,' he replies.

'You see, that's what I can't get my head around,' she says. 'You're the fifth person I've asked today, and each one gives me a different answer.'

*Why is an Essex Girl like a beer bottle?*
They're both empty from the neck up.

The doctor is explaining to Donna how nature adjusts certain physical disabilities. 'For example,' he says, 'if someone is blind, they develop a keen sense of hearing and touch. Similarly someone who is deaf will develop other senses.'

'I know what you mean,' says Donna. 'I've noticed that if a guy has one short leg, then the other one is always a bit longer.'

*Why did the Essex Girl go out with her purse open?*
Because she had heard there was going to be some change in the weather.

An Essex Girl marches into Basildon Library and tells the librarian: 'I want to complain about a book I took out last week. It has far too many characters, and there is no plot at all.'

'Ah!' says the librarian. 'Are you the person who took our phone directory?'

*What is an Essex Girl doing when she places her hands tightly over her ears?*
Trying to hold on to a thought.

*What do you call an Essex Girl with an IQ of 150?*
Basildon.

*Why was the Essex Girl so pleased to finish a jigsaw puzzle in nine months?*
Because on the box it said: '2 to 5 years'.

*How do an Essex Girl's brain cells die?*
Alone.

When one of the regular players is away on holiday, an Essex Girl is persuaded to join a pub quiz team to make up the numbers for one night only. The first question is: 'What's the capital of Slovenia?'

'OMG!' shrieks the Essex Girl. 'That's so easy. S.'

*What do you call an Essex Girl who has lost ninety per cent of her intelligence?*
Divorced.

*Why do Essex Girls wear earmuffs?*
To avoid the draught.

*How does an Essex Girl spell 'farm'?*
E-I-E-I-O.

*Why is an Essex Girl's brain the size of a pea in the morning?*
It swells at night.

*What do you call an Essex Boy with half a brain?*
Gifted.

Two Essex Girls are having an intellectual discussion about world affairs. Eventually one says to the other: 'So what's the right way to pronounce it, Iran or Iraq?'

*Why do Essex Girls always smile during light-ning storms?*
They think their picture is being taken.

An Essex Girl phones her boyfriend and wails: 'I'm doing a jigsaw puzzle and I can't fit any of the pieces together.'

'What's the puzzle of?' he asks.

'It's of a big cockerel,' she says, 'but I can't do it. Nuffink fits. Please come and help me.'

When he arrives, she shows him into the kitchen. 'The pieces are all over the kitchen table,' she moans. 'It's no good.'

Taking one look at the problem, he says: 'Babe, put the cornflakes back in the box.'

A girl arrives home from school. 'Mummy, Mummy!' she says excitedly. 'We did counting today and all the other kids could only count to five but I counted all the way to seven. Is that because I was born in Essex, Mummy?'

'Yes, darling,' says her mother. 'It's because you were born in Essex.'

The next day the girl comes home from school and shrieks: 'Mummy, Mummy, we were doing the alphabet today and all the other kids could only go up to F but I went all the way to H. Is that because I was born in Essex, Mummy?'

'Yes, darling,' says her mother. 'It's because you were born in Essex.'

The next day the girl gets home from school and says: 'Mummy, Mummy, we were doing PE today, and when we showered all the other girls had flat chests but I have my lovely 38Ds. Is that because I was born in Essex, Mummy?'

'No, darling,' says her mother. 'It's because you're twenty-seven.'

*Did you hear about the Essex Rubik's Cube?*
It's white on all sides and takes five minutes to solve.

*What's the difference between a supermarket trolley and an Essex Girl?*
A supermarket trolley has a mind of its own.

# LET'S TALK ABOUT ABOUT SEX

*What's the mating call of an Essex Girl?*
'I'm soooo drunk!'

At a Romford bar, a guy is eyeing up a girl who is wearing the tightest pair of leather pants he's ever seen. 'Oi, gorgeous,' he says. 'How do you get into those pants?'

'Well,' she replies, 'you could start by buying me a drink.'

*What do Essex Girls wear behind their ears to attract Essex Boys?*
Their heels.

*What's the quickest way to get into an Essex Girl's knickers?*
Pick them up off the floor.

*What's the difference between an Essex Boy and an Essex Girl?*
The Essex Girl has a higher sperm count.

An Essex Girl goes into a sex shop and asks for a vibrator. The man at the desk says: 'Choose from our range on the wall.'
'I'll take the red one,' she says.
He replies: 'That's a fire extinguisher.'

*Why don't Essex Girls use vibrators?*
They keep chipping their teeth.

*How does an Essex Girl turn the light out after sex?*
She shuts the car door.

*What do Essex Girls use for protection during sex?*
Bus shelters.

*Why do Essex Girls take the Pill?*
So they know what day of the week it is.

*Why did the Essex Girl stop taking the Pill?*
It kept falling out.

Not again!

Shelley goes to the doctor about an embarrassing rash. The doctor prescribes her a course of antibiotics and advises: 'Until you have finished the course and the rash has cleared up, you should avoid having relations.'

Shelley thinks about this for a moment and then asks: 'Does this mean my mum can't come round to dinner on Sunday?'

63

An Essex Girl goes into a pharmacy and asks for some condoms.

'What size?' asks the pharmacist.

'Oh, just mix them up,' she says. 'I'm not going steady with anyone right now.'

Why don't Essex Girls eat bananas?
They can't find the zips.

What's an Essex Girl's idea of foreplay?
Removing her knickers.

Did you hear about the vengeful Essex Girl who tried to blow up her boyfriend's car?
She burned her lips on the exhaust pipe.

How is an Essex Girl like a doorknob?
Everyone gets a turn.

What's the difference between an Essex Girl and a Kit-Kat?
You only get four fingers in a Kit-Kat.

Why do Essex Girls wear hoop earrings?
So they'll have somewhere to rest their ankles.

A young student picks up an Essex Girl in a nightclub and asks her out on a date. To impress her, he takes her to a smart restaurant, but is dismayed when she orders champagne and the most expensive dishes on the menu.

He asks her: 'Does your mother feed you like this at home?'

'No,' she says, 'but my mother's not looking to get laid.'

Three lads pick up three girls in a Romford nightclub, and they all head back to one of the girls' houses because her parents are away. There they pair off and go to different bedrooms.

In the first bedroom, the guy sees the girl getting undressed and exclaims: 'Bloody hell, what a big arse you've got!' She is furious and throws him out onto the landing.

In the second bedroom, the guy sees his girl undressing and says: 'Blimey! What enormous tits you've got! They're grotesque!' She is really angry and throws him out onto the landing.

A couple of minutes later the two lads are joined on the landing by the third boy. They say: 'Did you put your foot in it?'

'No,' he says, 'but I probably could have done!'

*What did the Essex Girl's right leg say to her left leg?*
Nothing. They've never met.

An Essex Girl walks into the doctor's surgery and asks him: 'Did I leave my panties here yesterday?'

'Er, no,' says the doctor, surprised by the question. 'I don't think so.'

'Oh, bother!' she says. 'I must have left them at the dentist's.'

A minibus full of Essex schoolgirls is involved in a crash and they all die. The next thing they know they are all at the entrance to heaven trying to get past St Peter at the Pearly Gates.

St Peter asks the first girl (from Canvey Island): 'Lorraine, have you ever had any contact with a man's thing?'

She giggles and shyly replies: 'Well, I once touched the head of one with the tip of my finger.'

'OK,' says St Peter, 'dip the tip of your finger in the Holy Water and pass through the gate.'

St Peter asks the next girl (from Basildon) the same question: 'Leanne, have you ever had any contact with a man's thing?'

The girl is a little reluctant but replies: 'Well, I did once fondle and stroke one.'

'OK,' says St Peter, 'dip your whole hand in the Holy Water and pass through the gate.'

All of a sudden there is a great deal of commotion in the line of girls, and a girl from Romford is trying to push her way to the front. When she gets there, St Peter says: 'Kerry! What seems to be the rush?'

The girl replies: 'If I'm going to have to gargle that Holy Water, I want to do it before Shazza sticks her arse in it!'

*Did you hear about the Essex Girl who thought Little Red Riding Hood was a novelty condom?*

*What happens when an Essex Girl has finished having sex with you?*
The next person in the queue taps you on the shoulder.

*What do you say to an Essex Girl who says 'no'?*
'Have another Lambrini.'

*What's the difference between an Essex Girl and a broom cupboard?*
Only two men can fit inside a broom cupboard at the same time.

*What's the difference between the Blackpool Tower and an Essex Girl?*
Not everyone's been up the Blackpool Tower.

*How can you tell if an Essex Girl has been in your fridge?*
By the lipstick stains on the cucumber.

*What's the difference between an Essex Girl and a bag of crisps?*
You only get one bang out of a bag of crisps.

Mikey is on a date with the easiest girl in Billericay. After they park the car, she quickly climbs into the back seat and encourages him to slip his hand inside her knickers. As the petting increases in intensity, she starts moaning with pleasure until she suddenly cries: 'Ow! Your ring is hurting me!'

'That's not my ring,' says Mikey. 'It's my watch!'

*Why do eighteen-year-old Essex Girls take sex education classes?*
To find out what they've been doing wrong for the past five years.

A King's Cross prostitute has a strict price list – £30 for sex in an alley, £60 for sex in a car and £90 for sex in bed.

One evening, a Scouser approaches her and gives her £30. She takes him to a dirty alley and they have sex.

An hour later, a Geordie approaches her and gives her £60. They climb into the back seat of his car and have sex.

An hour after that, an Essex Boy approaches her and hands her £90.

'At last, someone with class,' she says.

'Class my arse!' he says. 'I want it three times down the alley.'

*What does an Essex Girl say after having sex?*
    'So what team do you guys play for?'

An Essex Boy is chatting up a girl in a Southend night-club. He says to her: 'You remind me of my little toe.'

'Aah!' she says. 'Is that because I'm small and cute?'

'Nah,' he says, 'it's because I'll probably end up banging you on the coffee table.'

An Essex Girl and a Surrey Girl are discussing their boyfriends.

The Surrey Girl says: 'Last night I had three orgasms in a row.'

'I would be well jel,' replies the Essex Girl, 'but last night I had over thirty orgasms.'

'Gosh!' says the Surrey Girl. 'I never knew he was that good.'

'Oh!' says the Essex Girl. 'You mean with one guy?'

Dave says to Kev: 'I'm going to hold an orgy in my flat tonight. Are you up for it?'

'Too right I am!' says Kev excitedly. 'How many people are coming?'

Dave says: 'Three, if you bring your girlfriend.'

*Why aren't there many Essex Girl gymnasts?*
Because when they do the splits they stick to the floor.

*Why is an Essex Girl like rail tracks?*
Because she's been laid all over the country.

An Essex Boy and an Essex Girl are making out in his car when she says: 'Put your finger inside me.'

He does and then she says: 'Put another finger inside me.'

He puts in two fingers and she starts moaning with pleasure. 'Put your whole hand inside me,' she says.

'Now put both hands inside me!' she screams.

'Now clap your hands!' she gasps.

'I can't clap,' he protests.

'I know,' she smiles. 'Tight, aren't I?'

An Essex Girl goes into B&Q and tells one of the staff she needs a new door handle.

He fetches one and asks: 'You wanna screw for that?'

She looks around the store and says: 'No, but I'll blow ya for that shower unit over there.'

*What do an Essex Girl and a tortoise have in common?*
When they're on their back, they're f**ked.

*What is an Essex Girl's idea of real class?*
An onyx dildo.

Patrolling a lovers' lane in Epping Forest, a policeman spots a young couple sitting in their car with the interior light on. The young man is sitting in the driver's seat reading a magazine while the girl is sitting in the back seat doing her nails. Puzzled, the policeman taps on the window and asks the driver: 'What's going on?'

The driver winds down the window and answers: 'What does it look like? I'm reading this magazine.'

The policeman gestures towards the girl in the back and asks: 'And what's she doing?'

The young man glances over his shoulder and says: 'What does it look like? She's doing her nails.'

'How old are you?' the policeman asks the young man.

'I'm nineteen.'

'And how old is she?' continues the policeman.

The young man looks at his watch and says: 'In about eight minutes she'll be sixteen.'

*Did you hear about the Essex Girl who won't stand for oral sex?*
She prefers to kneel down for it.

---

An Essex Girl goes to the doctor for a check-up. He asks: 'Are you sexually active?'

'Sometimes,' she replies, 'but other times I just lie there.'

---

*How is an Essex Girl like a TV set?*
Any fool can turn her on.

An Essex Girl is having sex with her boyfriend for the first time. After a while he asks her to open her legs a bit wider.

She does so and they carry on, but a minute or so later he asks again: 'Darlin', can you open your legs a bit wider?'

Again she obliges but shortly afterwards he says: 'Darlin', a bit wider.'

She wriggles into position and they continue but thirty seconds later he begs: 'Darlin', can you just open your legs a little bit wider?'

'What are you trying to do?' she barks impatiently. 'Get your balls in, too?'

'No,' he says, 'I'm trying to get them out!'

*How is an Essex Girl like a vacuum cleaner?*
She sucks, blows, and finally gets laid in the
cupboard under the stairs.

*Why was the Essex Girl's nickname
'Workmate'?*
Because she accepted tools of all sizes.

*What's the difference between an Essex Girl
and a fridge?*
A fridge doesn't fart when you take your
meat out.

---

'You think I'm easy, don't ya?' says Paige to
her mother at the height of a family row. 'Well,
I'll have you know I've been out with dozens
of boys and I haven't let one of them shag me.'

'Really?' says her mother. 'And which one
was that?'

---

*What's an Essex Girl's favourite drink?*
7-Up.

Wayne goes straight down on his girlfriend one night,
so she slaps him round the face.

'Where's yer manners?' she says. 'Tits first!'

*What is a belly button for?*
It gives an Essex Girl somewhere to park her
gum on the way down.

Chantelle is taking her three-year-old son for a walk through the park in Southend when he spots two birds mating. 'What are they doing, Mummy?' he asks.

Feeling he's still too young to be told the facts of life, she says: 'Oh, they're making sandwiches, sweetheart.'

A few minutes later, the boy sees two dogs mating. He asks: 'What are they doing, Mummy?'

'Oh, they're making sandwiches, too.'

That night the boy is in bed when he hears noises coming from his mother's bedroom. Inquisitive, he quietly opens the door and sees Chantelle romping with her boyfriend. When she sees him, she cries out in horror: 'What do you want?'

'I know what you were doing!' he says. 'You were making sandwiches.'

She blushes and says: 'How can you tell?'

He replies: 'Because you've got mayonnaise all over your face.'

Santa asks the six-year-old daughter of an Essex Girl what she would like for Christmas.

'I want a Barbie and Action Man,' says the little girl.

'I thought Barbie came with Ken,' says Santa.

'No,' says the child. 'Barbie comes with Action Man. She fakes it with Ken.'

A policeman sees an Essex Girl crying in the street. 'What's happened?' he asks.

She sobs: 'A thief has just stolen £30 that I had hidden inside my knickers.'

'Did you try to stop him?' says the officer.

The Essex Girl replies: 'I didn't know he was after my money!'

An Essex Girl goes to a gynaecologist and tells him that she and her husband are desperate to start a family. 'We've been trying for months,' she says, 'but I just don't seem able to get pregnant.'

'I'm sure we can solve your problem,' says the gynaecologist. 'If you'll just take off your panties and get up on the examining table . . .'

'Well, OK,' says the Essex Girl, 'but to be honest I'd rather have my husband's baby.'

*What's the difference between butter and an Essex Girl?*
Butter is difficult to spread.

*What do you call an Essex Girl who has sex with two men in one day?*
Frigid.

*What's the difference between an Essex Girl and a payphone?*
Only one person at a time can use a payphone.

A surgeon goes to see his Essex Girl patient on the day after her operation. Sitting up in her hospital bed, she asks him: 'How long will it be before I can have sex again?'

'Oh,' says the surgeon, taken aback. 'I must confess I hadn't really thought about it. You're the first patient ever to ask that after a tonsillectomy.'

*What do Essex Girls have against condoms?*
*Their cheeks.*

Shelley is well drunk after a Friday night out in Brentwood and is stark naked when she falls into a taxi and asks the driver to take her home. As they go along the road, she notices that he keeps looking at her through his rear-view mirror.

'What you lookin' at?' she snaps. 'Why are you staring at me?'

'You're naked,' says the cabbie, glancing again in the mirror. 'How are you going to pay the fare?'

With that, Shelley opens her legs, puts her feet up on the front seat, grins and says: 'Does this answer your question?'

Still looking in his mirror, he says: 'Got anything smaller?'

An Essex Girl walks into her local dry cleaners. She puts a dress on the counter and tells the elderly sales assistant: 'I'll be back tomorrow afternoon to pick up my dress.'

'Come again?' says the assistant, cupping her ear.

'No,' says the Essex Girl. 'This time it's mayonnaise.'

# MODERN TECHNOLOGY

*Why don't Essex Girls have jobs as lift operators?*
They can't remember the route.

*What do Essex Girls and computers have in common?*
You don't know how much either of them means to you until they go down on you.

Mark was very excited when he got an AM radio. It took him six weeks before he realised he could also play it in the afternoon.

*How do you know an Essex Girl has been
using her iPad?*
There's Tipp-Ex on the screen.

*Why was the Essex Girl searching for the
reverse button on her computer?*
She'd been told to back up at the end of
each day.

Why did the Essex Boy try to make his internet
password 'MickeyMinnieDonaldPlutoGoofy'?
  Because he read it had to have at least five
characters.

An Essex Boy is sharing a flat with a Surrey Boy.

One day the Surrey Boy arrives home to find the Essex Boy propping up the washing machine on one side with two bricks.

'What are you doing?' asks the Surrey Boy.

The Essex Boy replies: 'I'm doing the washing at 30 degrees.'

*Did you hear about the Essex Girl who almost killed her toy poodle?*
*She tried to insert batteries.*

An Essex Girl texts her friend to ask: 'What does "idk" stand for?'

The friend texts back: 'I don't know.'

'OMG!' replies the Essex Girl. 'No one does!'

Tracey says to her flatmate Paige: 'Set the alarm for seven in the morning.'

'Why?' says Paige. 'There's only two of us.'

An Essex Girl buys a bathtub, but the next day she goes back to the shop to complain that it emptied automatically after she filled it up with water.

'All you need is a plug,' says the shopkeeper.

'Oh,' says the Essex Girl, 'I didn't know it was electric.'

A power cut at Lakeside left Sharon stuck on an escalator for two hours. When she was finally rescued her boyfriend asked her: 'Why didn't you walk down?'

She said: 'Because I was going up, silly!'

A young woman moved into a furnished flat in Chelmsford. All the kitchen appliances worked perfectly, there was a nice sofa, the bathroom was clean – in fact the only downside was that she couldn't get a picture on the portable TV.

So after a couple of hours she phoned the landlord, who suggested: 'Have you tried switching it on and off a few times? It's not a new set, and sometimes these old ones can be a bit temperamental.'

'OK, I'll try that,' she said, and hung up.

She switched it on and off, but still there was no picture.

An hour later, she phoned him again. 'I still can't get a picture on the TV,' she said.

He suggested: 'Have you tried twisting the indoor aerial? You might get a better picture if it's facing in another direction.'

'OK, I'll try that,' she said, and hung up. But even after turning the aerial in every conceivable direction she still couldn't get a picture.

Half an hour later, she phoned him again: 'I'm still not having any luck with getting a picture on the TV. I've tried everything you've suggested. I don't know what's wrong with it.'

'Very well,' sighed the landlord. 'I'll come round and have a look at it.'

An hour later, he arrived at the flat. She let him in and, pointing at the blank screen, said: 'I really hope you can fix it. I'm lost without a TV.'

'I can see straight away why you haven't managed to get a picture,' he said.

'Oh, why's that?'

'Because that's the microwave. The portable TV is in the bedroom!'

Nicola had a terrifying experience riding a horse. For no apparent reason, the beast started to get wildly out of control.

She desperately tried to hang on to the reins but the horse was so frisky that eventually she was thrown off. As she fell, her foot caught in the stirrup and her head bounced repeatedly on the ground with the horse refusing to stop or even slow down.

Finally she was rescued when the manager of Poundland came out and unplugged the machine.

*Why did the Essex Girl paint her sundial with luminous paint?*
So she could tell the time at night.

Jade goes to B&Q and asks: 'Have you got a box that is two inches high, two inches wide and fifty feet long?'

'Why do you want a box like that?' asks the sales assistant.

'Well,' explains Jade, 'my neighbour moved away and forgot some things, so he asked me to send him his garden hose.'

Alone and bored in her flat one night, an Essex Girl decides to do something spontaneous. So she goes to her local Blockbuster with the intention of renting an adult video. She scans the shelves and eventually selects a film that sounds suitably sexy.

Then she goes home, pours herself a large glass of Chardonnay and settles back to enjoy an evening of erotica.

But when she puts the video into the machine, there is nothing but static, so she calls the store to complain.

She says: 'I just rented an adult film from you but there's nothing on the tape but static.'

'Sorry about that,' says the sales assistant. 'We've had problems with some of those tapes. What title did you rent?'

The Essex Girl replies: 'It's called *Head Cleaner*.'

Susie meets Donna in the street and asks: 'Why ain't you been texting me lately? I haven't heard from you for three days.'

Susie replies: 'Because since it was stolen, you ain't got a phone.'

'I know,' says Donna, 'but you have!'

An Essex Boy and a Surrey Boy go parachuting for the first time. They jump from the plane together, but when the Surrey Boy pulls the parachute cord nothing happens. He then pulls the emergency cord, but still his chute doesn't open.

Seeing this, the Essex Boy says: 'Oh, so you wanna race, do you?'

*Did you hear about the Essex Girl who bought half a dozen iPads to deal with her periods?*

Danny buys a smoke alarm for his Billericay flat. After fixing it to the ceiling, he reads the instructions, which say: 'Now test your alarm.'

So he sets fire to his sofa.

Three female students at Chelmsford University are given the job of measuring the height of the campus's new flagpole. So they get a ladder and while two hold the bottom, the third girl tentatively starts to climb. They are being watched by a male engineering student who, seeing their struggles, takes the flagpole out of its base, lays it on the ground and measures it.

The girls look at each other and groan: 'Typical useless engineer! He gives us the length when we want the height!'

## MODERN TECHNOLOGY

*Did you hear about the Essex Girl who was puzzled because she kept getting text messages from some guy called Lol?*

An Essex Boy asked his Essex Girl sister to put his laptop in hibernate mode. Two months later, he's still getting the twigs and leaves out.

---

An Essex Girl goes into a curtain store and orders a pair of curtains. 'What width do you need?' asks the sales assistant.

'Fifteen inches,' replies the Essex Girl.

'That sounds rather small. What room are they for?'

'They're not for a room, stupid,' beams the Essex Girl. 'They're for my computer screen.'

The sales assistant looks puzzled. 'But computers don't need curtains . . .'

'Helloooo!' says the Essex Girl. 'I've got Windows!'

---

Carol and Gemma take an item along to *The Antiques Roadshow*.

'Where did you find this?' asks the expert, examining the large metal box.

'Oh, it's been in the attic for years,' says Carol.

'Have you got insurance?' asks the expert.

'Do you think we should?' says Gemma brightly.

'Yes, you're definitely going to need it,' says the expert. 'This is your cold water tank.'

# R IS
## FOR
# RELATIONSHIPS

*What do you give an Essex Girl before you*
*start going out with her?*
A full medical.

An Essex Girl is walking with her boyfriend along the seafront at Southend when she looks up to see a seagull flying overhead. As she does so, the bird drops its load directly on to her.

She turns to her boyfriend and says: "Ere, Dave, it's a good job I had my mouth open or that would've hit me right in the face!'

An Essex Girl and her boyfriend are sitting in a hot tub at their holiday apartment in Magaluf. After a while she says to him: 'Is it true that if you pull your finger out I'll sink?'

An Essex Girl and her boyfriend are chatting in a bar. He says: 'I see Christmas Day is on a Friday this year.'

'Well,' she says, 'I hope it's not the 13th!'

Paige tells Becky that she's split up with her boyfriend.

'Why?' asks Becky. 'He's reem.'

'Yeah,' says Paige, 'but I saw him naked last night for the first time and, you know, he doesn't look so good without his wallet.'

*Why did the Essex wife ask the doctor for some cream?*
She was worried about the seven-year itch.

Mikey is suspicious after hearing his girlfriend Janine chatting on the phone, so he decides to confront her. He asks her: 'Who was that you were talking to on the phone? Is there someone else?'

'Course not,' she says. 'Do you think I'd be hanging out with a loser like you if there was someone else?'

*What did the Essex Girl say after being told
she was pregnant?*
'Are you sure it's mine?'

A man arrives home from work to find his young
Essex Girl wife sliding down the banister.
'What are you doing?' he asks.
She replies: 'Just heating up dinner.'

*Why did God create Essex Girls?*
Because sheep can't fetch beer from the
fridge.

On the first night of their honeymoon in Florida, a guy slips out of the hotel room to buy his Essex Girl bride a single red rose. He returns to find her naked on the bed with four male members of the hotel staff. She is screwing one, giving oral sex to another and giving hand jobs to two more.

'What the hell's going on?' demands the groom.

'What's the big deal?' says his Essex Girl bride, coming up for air. 'You always knew I was a flirt.'

To spice up their sex life, Tracy and Ray buy a manual. After reading it from cover to cover, he tells her: 'Trace, I want to perform oral sex with you like it says in the book, but the trouble is, babe, it smells pretty bad down there. Why don't you buy some of that special feminine deodorant spray?'

'OK, darlin',' she says, and heads off to the shops.

She returns forty minutes later, very excited. 'You should see the flavours they have!' she says. 'Strawberry, cherry, banana . . .'

'Great! What flavour did you get?'

'Tuna.'

*How do you get an Essex Girl to marry you?*
Tell her she's pregnant.

Tina wasn't the most accomplished of cooks. In fact, her husband said she was such a bad cook their cat only had three lives left.

Wounded by the insults, she ambitiously decided to bake her husband a birthday cake. She asked her friend Jo for a recipe and went to Romford Tesco's for all the ingredients.

She had never baked a cake before but was determined to prove herself. Jo said she would pop round later in case the cake needed urgent repairs.

When Jo came to call, she was half expecting to see a couple of fire engines outside the house, but instead everything seemed calm.

'Well,' she said. 'How did it go?'

'It was easy,' said Tina. 'I don't know what all the fuss is about. Anyone can bake a cake. Come into the kitchen and I'll show you my masterpiece.'

Jo studied the cake on the kitchen table and was impressed.

'It looks good,' she said. 'I'm sure Simon will love it. One thing though: where are the candles?'

'Oh,' said Tina. 'They melted in the oven.'

An Essex Girl and her boyfriend are walking along the seafront at Westcliff when he turns to her and says: 'Look, a dead bird.'

She looks up to the sky and says: 'Where?'

Chardonnay and Charlie have a row. The next day, she sends him a blank text. When he asks why, she texts back: 'Because I'm not talking to you.'

*How can you tell when an Essex Girl is dating?*
By the buckle print on her forehead.

Jez gives Leanne a small diamond. 'You said I was getting an engagement ring!' she moans. 'This is just an unmounted stone.'

'Don't worry,' he says. 'It'll be mounted the day after you are.'

When her husband arrives home from work, Alex hugs him and tells him excitedly: 'I'm pregnant – and it's twins!'

'How do you know it's twins?' he asks.

'Well,' she explains, 'I went to the pharmacy and bought the two-pack pregnancy test kit. And both tests came out positive.'

An Essex Girl shows her boyfriend the pregnancy test she took. The result is positive.

'What do you think?' he asks tentatively. 'Should we keep it?'

'Not much point,' she says. 'You can only use them once.'

---

An Essex Girl goes to the council to register for child benefit.

'How many children do you have?' asks the council officer.

'Ten,' replies the Essex Girl.

'Ten?!' says the council officer. 'What are their names?'

'Wayne, Wayne, Wayne, Wayne, Wayne, Wayne, Wayne, Wayne, Wayne and Wayne.'

'Doesn't that get confusing?'

'Naah,' says the Essex Girl, 'it's OK cos if they're out playing in the street I just have to shout "WAAAYNE, YER DINNER'S READY!" or "WAAAYNE, GO TO BED NOW" and they all do it.'

'But what if you want to speak to one individually?' asks the puzzled council officer.

'That's easy,' says the Essex Girl. 'I just use their last names.'

An Essex Boy comes home from signing on and finds that his girlfriend is jumping up and down excitedly.

'What's happened?' he asks. 'Have the lottery numbers come up?'

'Nah,' she says, 'it's our Darren.'

'What, has he come top of the class at something?'

'Nah, it's better than that. He's got his first Asbo!'

*What did the Essex Girl say to her boyfriend when she knocked over his priceless Ming vase?*

'It's OK, I'm not hurt.'

An Essex Girl goes into Boots and tells the sales assistant: 'I want to buy some deodorant for my boyfriend.'

'Does he use the ball kind?' asks the assistant.

'Nah,' says the Essex Girl. 'It's the kind for under his arms.'

---

Essex Girl Candice had injured her right shoulder at the gym. It was causing her considerable pain, so she told her boyfriend: 'Until it gets better, you'll have to do all the jobs around the flat.'

'Like what?' he said.

'Well, the cooking for a start.'

'No problem. I'll just get a KFC bucket.'

'And the washing,' she added.

'I'll just buy some new gear to tide me through.'

'And the hoovering.'

'You know I hate hoovering!' he whined.

'Well, somebody's got to do it, otherwise the place will be a pig sty, and I can't use my right arm for the next few months.'

'Bleedin' 'ell, Candice. What are we going to do?'

Just then she had a brainwave. And the next day she went into Currys and asked for a left-handed vacuum cleaner.

---

An Essex Girl and an Essex Boy are playing hide-and-seek. She sends him a text: 'If you can find me, you can have me. If you can't find me, I'm in the shed.'

With his girlfriend eight months pregnant, Romford Ray is becoming increasingly desperate for sex. One night, as he gazes longingly at Tracy in bed, she finally takes pity on him, reaches into her handbag and pulls out £30 in notes. ''Ere,' she says, 'take this to the woman at number 44. Her name's Jackie. She'll let you sleep with her for thirty quid. But remember, this is a one-off. Don't even think about trying it again.'

'Thanks, babe,' he says. 'You're a life-saver. I can't think of any other woman who'd do that for her man. What have I done to deserve you?' Then he kisses her tenderly on the forehead, gets dressed and rushes out of the house before she changes her mind.

Five minutes later, he returns, hands the £30 back to Tracy and says dejectedly: 'It's not enough. She says she wants £50.'

'The bitch!' rages Tracy. 'When she was pregnant and her boyfriend came over here, I only charged him thirty!'

A woman in her late thirties was asked to give a talk on the power of prayer to her local Essex women's group. With her husband sitting in the audience, she recounted how they had turned to God when her husband suffered an unfortunate accident.

'Six months ago,' she began, 'my husband Tony was knocked off his motorbike and his scrotum was smashed. The pain was excruciating and the doctors didn't know if they could help him. They warned that our lives might never be the same again. Tony was unable to get close to either me or the children and every move caused him enormous discomfort. It meant we could no longer touch him around the scrotum.

'So we prayed that the doctors would be able to repair him. Fortunately our prayers were answered and they were able to piece together the crushed remnants of Tony's scrotum and wrap wire around it to hold it in place. They said he should make a complete recovery and regain full use of his scrotum.'

As the audience burst into spontaneous applause, a lone man walked up to the stage. He announced: 'Good afternoon. My name is Tony, and I just want to tell my wife once again that the word is "sternum".'

*What does an Essex Girl make for dinner?*
Reservations.

Mick calls Sharon from hospital and tells her that his finger has been cut off in an accident at work.

'OMG!' cries Sharon. 'The whole finger?'

'No,' says Mick, 'the one next to it.'

An Essex Girl and her boyfriend are flying to Ibiza.

Fifteen minutes into the flight, the captain comes on the PA and announces: 'We've lost engine number one, so I'm afraid we'll be thirty minutes late landing in Ibiza.'

Five minutes later, he announces: 'We've now lost engine number two, so I'm afraid we'll be an hour late landing in Ibiza.'

Five minutes later, he announces: 'I've never known a flight like this. We've lost engine number three as well, so I'm afraid we'll be two hours late landing in Ibiza.'

Hearing this, the Essex Girl turns to her boyfriend and says: 'I hope we don't lose engine number four or we're gonna be up here all night.'

Mandy and Wayne go on their first date. When he turns up, the first thing she asks him is: 'Are you a vampire?'

'No,' he replies, puzzled.

'So,' she says, 'you can see your reflection and still you come out looking like that?!'

Sharon and Kev are being kept awake at night by their neighbours' dog barking loudly in the garden. Eventually Tracy says: 'This is doin' my 'ead in!' And she jumps out of bed and storms downstairs.

Five minutes later, she returns to bed.

'What've you been doing?' asks Kev.

Sharon says: 'I've put the bloody dog in our garden. Let's see how they like it!'

Jenny persuades her boyfriend to take her to a restaurant. But she's not used to eating out and doesn't know what to order.

'Why don't you just have what I have?' he suggests.

'What and leave you hungry?' she says. 'No, I couldn't do that!'

Hearing that Jamie Oliver has opened a new restaurant in Chelmsford, an Essex Girl begs her boyfriend to take her there. As they study the menu, he asks her: 'Do you fancy molasses?'

'Bee-ayve!' she squeals. 'I'm not eating any part of a mole!'

To celebrate their first wedding anniversary, an Essex Boy decides to cook his wife a special meal. He tells her to go and sit in the lounge and relax watching TV while he prepares dinner.

Forty-five minutes pass and she starts to feel hungry. So she calls through to the kitchen: 'Is everything OK, hun?'

'Yes,' he replies, sounding a little harassed. 'It won't be long.'

She thinks it best not to interfere and sits down again in front of the TV.

Another hour passes, and she is starting to feel distinctly light-headed. 'Any idea when dinner will be ready, hun?' she calls out.

'Any minute now,' he replies, still sounding frantic.

Another half-hour passes, and finally she can bear it no longer. She barges into the kitchen to find the room in a terrible mess and the dinner not yet even in the oven.

'What's going on?' she demands.

'Sorry it's taken longer than I thought,' he says. 'But I had to refill the pepper shaker.'

'How could that take over two hours?' she asks.

'Well,' he explains, 'it's not easy stuffing the pepper through those stupid little holes.'

---

An Essex Girl decides to paint the apartment she shares with her boyfriend. She takes a day off work to get it done and blitzes through the DIY. When her boyfriend gets home, he pops his head round the door to admire her handi-work, but is puzzled by what she is wearing.

He asks her: 'Why are you wearing a ski jacket over your military coat?'

'Because, silly,' she explains, 'it says on the paint tin: "For best results, put on two coats."'

---

Tracy says to Ray: 'Ere, I had a funny dream last night. I was at this auction for penises. The big ones sold for £1,000 and the tiny ones for £50.'

'What about one my size?' asks Ray.

'There weren't any bids for it!' laughs Tracy.

Ray feels humiliated by the jibe, so he plans his revenge. The next morning he tells Tracy: 'I had a funny dream last night. I was at an auction for vaginas. The really tight ones sold for £1,000 and the loose ones for £50.'

'What about one like mine?' asks Tracy.

Ray says: 'That's where they held the auction.'

Chantelle brings her new boyfriend home after a night out in Chelmsford. Her parents are in bed so she tells him to keep the noise down. He is desperate to use the toilet, but rather than send him upstairs and risk waking her parents, she tells him to use the kitchen sink.

A few minutes later, he pokes his head around the lounge door.

'Have you finished?' she whispers.

'Yeah,' he replies. 'Got any paper?'

After they'd been dating for six months, an Essex Girl says to her boyfriend: 'I'm bored with our sex life. It's always the same. Why don't we do something different? Why don't we try the "other hole"?'

'Yuk! No way!' he says. 'And risk you getting pregnant?'

---

Janine and Frank are watching an item on the evening news about a guy who is threatening to jump off the roof of a building. Frank says to Janine: 'I bet you a tenner he jumps.'

'OK, you're on,' says Janine.

A minute later, the man jumps and Janine hands over the £10.

'Listen,' says Frank, 'I can't take your money. You see, I watched this story on the lunchtime news and so I saw the guy jump then.'

'I watched the lunchtime news, too,' says Janine. 'I just didn't think the bloke would jump twice in one day.'

*Why did the Essex Girl put lipstick on her forehead?*
She wanted to make up her mind.

*What goes blonde, brunette, blonde, brunette?*
An Essex Girl doing naked cartwheels.

*How do you tickle an Essex Girl?*
Say: 'Gucci, Gucci, Gucci.'

*Why didn't the Essex Girl want a window seat on the plane?*
She'd just blow-dried her hair and didn't want it blown around too much.

An Essex Girl rushes into a hospital A&E department late one night with the tip of her index finger shot off.

'How did this happen?' asks the doctor.

'My boyfriend has dumped me and so I was trying to kill myself,' replies the Essex Girl.

'You mean you tried to commit suicide by shooting your finger off?' asks the doctor in disbelief.

'No, silly!' smiles the Essex Girl. 'First I put the gun to my chest, but then I thought: I just paid ten grand for these breast implants, I'm not shooting myself in the chest.'

'So then what?'

'Then I put the gun in my mouth, but I thought: I just paid five grand to get my teeth whitened and straightened, I'm not shooting myself in the mouth.'

'So what did you do?'

'Then I put the gun to my ear, and I thought: this is going to make a really loud noise. So I put my finger in the other ear before I pulled the trigger.'

---

An interviewer asks the Essex Girl glamour model: 'When you're photographed, do they use airbrush on you?'

'Yeah,' she says. 'And straighteners.'

---

Baz says to Daz: 'You know how my girlfriend wears fake nails, fake eyelashes, fake hair extensions and a fake tan?'

'Yeah.'

'Well, I'm starting to worry her orgasms are fake, too.'

An Essex Girl keeps complaining to her mother about getting terrible headaches, and theorises that her 'Croydon facelift' hairstyle may be to blame. But her mother shakes her head knowingly and says: 'How many times have I told you? When you get out of bed, it's feet first!'

*How do you know when an Essex Girl has had an orgasm?*
*She drops her nail file.*

*Why don't Essex Girls wear red lipstick?*
Because red means stop.

*Why do Essex Girls wash their hair in the kitchen sink?*
Because that's where you're supposed to wash vegetables.

---

An Essex Girl tells her boyfriend she is going off to have a vajazzle.

'What's a vajazzle?' he asks.

'It's where they put sequins all over a c\*\*t,' she replies.

'Oh,' he says. 'So you're going to be on *Strictly Come Dancing*?'

---

*Why do Essex Girls wear hair extensions?*
To hide the air valve.

*Why did the Essex Girl want iron breast implants?*
So she could show her mettle.

Essex Girl Stacey is knocked down by a car. As she lies unconscious by the roadside, she feels herself drifting through a long, dark tunnel towards a bright white light, where she meets God.

'It's not your time to die yet,' says God. 'You have another fifty or sixty years to live.' So she goes back to earth and makes a complete recovery.

Stacey is so grateful for her lucky escape that she decides to turn her life around. The first thing she does is go to the doctors to reverse all the plastic surgery she has had done over the years. Her trout pout lips are restored to their original size, her £8,000 boobs are reduced dramatically and she even stops applying the spray tan.

Happy with her new, natural look, she is leaving home one morning when she fails to notice a speeding car and is run over.

She finds herself before God once more, but this time she realises she is dead.

Furious, she yells at him: ''Ere, you said I'd have another fifty or sixty years.'

An embarrassed God apologises: 'I'm so sorry, I just didn't recognise you.'

---

'You look different today, Trace,' says Sharon. 'Your hair is extra curly, and you have this wide-eyed look? What is it – special curlers, Botox . . .?'

'Neither,' says Tracey. 'My dildo shorted out this morning.'

---

*Why do Essex Girls wear so much hairspray?*
So they can catch some of the things that go over their heads.

Ray says to Dave: 'I think Tracy's been overdoing it with the spray tan. She's now so orange that when we have sex she counts as one of my five a day!'

*Why did the Essex Girl stand in front of the mirror with her eyes closed?*
She wanted to see what she looked like asleep.

*What did the Essex Girl get on her maths exam?*
Nail varnish.

An Essex Girl is sitting in a Romford beauty salon listening intently to her iPod. The stylist notices that throughout the treatment the girl keeps wearing her headphones. Eventually when she dozes off, the stylist, curious as to what the Essex Girl is listening to, gently removes the headphones and hears: 'Breathe in, breathe out, breathe in . . .'

*How do you get an Essex Girl to burn her ear?*
Phone her while she's ironing.

*How do you get an Essex Girl to burn her ear twice?*
Phone her again while she's ironing.

*What's orange and sounds like a parrot?*
Half of Essex.

A woman from Dagenham bought some designer label clothes in a Bond Street store. She flashed her credit card, but because the bill was over £500 the store manager needed to run some checks before accepting payment.

'Can you give me the name and address of your bank, please?' he asked.

'Barclays, 227 Heathway,' she replied.

'And can you tell me your street name?'

'I don't have a street name,' she trilled. 'My friends just call me Sharon.'

*Why do Essex Girls have TGIF on their shoes?*
Toes go in first.

*Why do Essex Girls have TGIF on their shirts?*
Tits go in front.

*What's the difference between an Essex Girl and an inflatable doll?*
About two cans of hairspray.

On a visit to an Essex Girl's flat, her friend asks: 'Why have you got that huge picture of yourself above the wash basin in the bathroom?'

'Oh,' says the Essex Girl, 'my bathroom mirror broke, and I didn't want to buy a new one.'

An Essex Girl received a scarf for Christmas. But she took it back to the shop because it was too tight.

*Why do Essex Girls wear earrings?*
They want to look like their fathers.

---

Mandy says to Ray: 'I'm not happy with my boobs. I want to have implants.'

'You don't need implants, babe,' he says. 'I know a much cheaper way of doing it.'

'Like what?'

'All you need to do,' he says, 'is rub toilet paper between them.'

'And will that make my boobs bigger?'

'I don't know, but it worked for your arse!'

---

An Essex Girl goes to the doctor and says: 'Doctor, while I was washing my hair this morning I accidentally spilt a bottle of revitalising shampoo (with added Omega-3 to preserve my natural colour) down the plughole and I ended up swallowing a little. Will I die?'

The doctor smiles: 'Well, everyone is going to die eventually.'

'Oh my God!' shrieks the Essex Girl. 'Everyone? What have I done?'

*What's an Essex Girl's idea of natural childbirth?*
No make-up.

---

An Essex Girl is tottering down the road in a short leather skirt and designer high heels and carrying a pig under her arm.

A man calls out: 'Where did you get that?'

The pig answers: 'I won her in a raffle.'

*What does the label in an Essex Girl's*
*knickers say?*
NEXT.

*What does it mean if you see an Essex Girl*
*with square boobs?*
She forgot to take the Kleenex out of the
box.

An Essex Girl asks her boyfriend: 'Do you think I could be on *Britain's Next Top Model*?'

'No,' he says. 'I don't think so.'

'Why not?' she demands. 'I've got seven Next tops!'

# ESSEX GIRLS
## AND
## FRIENDS

An Essex Girl is enjoying a few Lambrinis at a friend's house one evening when it starts to rain heavily. As the weather deteriorates still further, the friend says to her: 'Why don't you stay here for the night and go home in the morning?'

At this, the Essex Girl rushes out of the door and returns an hour later, soaked to the skin and carrying a small bag.

'Where did you run off to?' asks the friend.

The Essex Girl replies: 'I went home to get my pyjamas.'

Kelly decides to redecorate the bedroom of her Billericay flat. She doesn't know how many rolls of wallpaper she'll need but she remembers that Tracey next door has recently done the same job and the two rooms are identical in size.

'Trace,' she says, 'how many rolls of wallpaper did you buy for your bedroom?'

'Eight,' answers Tracey.

So Kelly buys eight rolls of wallpaper and does the job, but at the end she has two rolls left over.

The next day she sees her neighbour in the street.

'Trace,' she says, 'I bought eight rolls of wallpaper for the bedroom, but I've got two left over.'

'Shuuut uuup!' says Tracey. 'So did I.'

An Essex Girl and a Scots Girl are talking one day. The Scots Girl says that her boyfriend had a slight dandruff problem, but she gave him 'Head and Shoulders' and it cleared it up.

The Essex Girl asks inquisitively: 'How do you give shoulders?'

*Did you hear about the helicopter that landed at Southend Airport?*
Two girls from the snack bar went out and threw it bits of bread.

Mandy and Stacey are waiting at a bus stop. A bus pulls up, and Mandy asks the driver: 'Will this bus take me to Romford Station?'

'No, sorry,' says the driver.

Stacey smiles sweetly and asks: 'Will it take me?'

---

At an Essex dinner party a few years back, the guests were discussing who was more trustworthy: men or women. One male guest was particularly outspoken on the matter, insisting: 'No woman can keep a secret.'

'That's so not true,' said the woman sitting opposite him. 'I've kept my age a secret since I was twenty.'

'You'll let it slip one day,' said the man.

'I so won't,' she said. 'When a woman has kept a secret for eighteen years, she can keep it forever.'

---

If an Essex Girl and a Surrey Girl jumped off the roof of a tower block at the same time, who would hit the ground first?

The Surrey Girl – because the Essex Girl would have to stop to ask for directions.

A group of Essex Girls appear in court on a public disorder charge. Their ringleader, Callie, is in the dock first. The magistrate says to her: 'Is it true that on April 22nd you committed an act of gross indecency with a one-legged dwarf and a man in a Batman costume on the roof of a white stretch limousine while travelling along Brentwood High Street at 60mph?'

The Essex Girl says: 'What was the date again?'

*What do you call a dozen Essex Girls sitting in a circle?*
A dope ring.

Two Essex Girls and a Surrey Girl are walking along Southend Beach when a seagull craps on one of the Essex Girls.

'I'll go and get some toilet paper,' says the Surrey Girl helpfully.

'And they say we're stupid!' says one Essex Girl to the other as the Surrey Girl disappears from view. 'By the time she gets back, that seagull will be miles away!'

---

Sharon and Tracey visit Battersea Dogs Home and each return home with a puppy from the same litter. Their excitement soon turns to confusion, however, when Sharon exclaims: 'Oh no! How are we going to tell them apart?'

They discuss the problem for over an hour until Tracey finally suggests: 'Why don't we tie a red bow around my puppy and a blue one around yours?'

'That's an amazing idea!' says Sharon. 'Why didn't I think of that?'

So they tie the different coloured ribbons around the puppies' necks, but the next day they arrive home to find that the puppies have pulled the ribbons off while playing.

'I'm so not sure which is my puppy,' says Sharon. 'What are we going to do?'

'OK,' says Tracey. 'We need to find a better way of telling them apart.'

After another two hours of brainstorming, Tracey suggests tying a small name tag around the neck of her puppy.

'That's another amazing idea!' says Sharon. 'Why didn't I think of that?'

So Tracey attaches a name tag to one of the puppies, but the next day the girls arrive home to find the detached tag lying on the kitchen floor.

'I can't take this no more,' says Sharon. 'My brain's going to explode. How are we ever going to tell them apart?'

'There must be some way,' Tracey muses.

'Well if there is, I can't think of it,' sighs Sharon desolately.

'I suppose,' says Tracey hesitantly, 'you could always take the black-and-white puppy and I'll have the brown one.'

---

An Essex Girl goes to the cinema in Stratford but sees a poster outside saying 'Under-16 not admitted'. So she goes home and phones fifteen of her friends.

---

On a Club 18–30 holiday in Greece, two Essex Girls become detached from the rest of their group and find themselves stuck in a dark cave. 'I can't see anything,' says one, panicking. 'Have you got a match?'

Her friend strikes the match against the wall of the cave but nothing happens. 'That's odd,' she says. 'This match worked fine this morning.'

*What do you call a Surrey Girl between two Essex Girls?*
An interpreter.

---

An angry farmer spots three young women – a Surrey Girl, a Kent Girl and an Essex Girl – helping themselves to his apples and then sneaking into his barn where, out of his view, they hide in three sacks. Wielding a sharp pitchfork, he marches into the barn to search for the culprits.

Soon he spots the three sacks with their suspicious bulges. He prods the first sack and the Surrey Girl says, 'Miaow.' So he thinks it's just a cat.

Then he prods the second sack and the Kent Girl says, 'Woof, woof.' So the farmer thinks the sack contains a dog.

Finally, he prods the third sack and the Essex Girl says, 'Potatoes.'

---

An Essex Girl, a Surrey Girl and a Kent Girl compete in the breaststroke division of an English Channel swimming competition. The Surrey Girl finishes first, the Kent Girl is second and the Essex Girl trails in third and last – over five hours later. She is completely exhausted. After being revived with blankets and drinks, she remarks: 'I don't want to complain, but I'm pretty sure those other two girls used their arms.'

Chardonnay and Leanne are chatting about their weekends. Chardonnay says: 'My boyfriend came round last night.'

'Oh,' says Leanne. 'I didn't even know he'd been in a coma.'

During a drunken girls' night out, Amie dares Sam to go shoplifting.

'You wouldn't have the bottle,' sneers Amie.

'Oh no?' retaliates Sam. 'You're so bloody up yourself, you are! I'll show you who's got bottle! I'll go shoplifting all right. You bloody wait and see!'

So the next day Sam goes on the internet, puts items in her online shopping basket and then logs off without paying.

Two Essex Girls fall down a well.

One says: 'It's dark down here, innit?'

'I dunno,' says the other. 'I can't see a thing.'

---

Searching for a Christmas tree, two Essex Girls venture deep into a Norwegian forest. After hours of braving sub-zero temperatures and a biting wind, one girl turns to the other and announces wearily: 'I'm chopping down the next tree I see. I don't care if it's decorated or not.'

---

*How do you keep a group of Essex Girls occupied for hours?*

Tell them to count the steps on an escalator.

... 14,324, 14,325 ...

Three people are stranded on an island – a Surrey Girl, a Geordie Girl and an Essex Girl.

The Surrey Girl stares out over the water to the mainland and estimates that it is about twenty miles to shore. So she announces: 'I'm going to try to swim to shore.' But after ten miles, she starts to feel really tired and, unable to continue, she sadly drowns.

Meanwhile the Geordie Girl thinks to herself: 'I wonder if she made it. I guess it's better to try to get to the mainland than stay here and starve.'

So she attempts to swim to shore. She is a stronger swimmer than the Surrey Girl but even so, after fifteen miles, she is exhausted and incapable of continuing. She, too, sadly drowns.

Back on the island the Essex Girl thinks: 'I wonder if they made it! I think I'd better try to swim to the mainland, too.'

So she swims out five miles, ten miles, fifteen miles, nineteen miles from the island. The shore of the mainland is now in sight, but then she thinks to herself: 'I'm just too tired to go on!' So she swims back to the island.

*How many Essex Girls does it take to play hide-and-seek?*
*One.*

Sharon meets Tina in a bar. Sharon says: 'I hear you've broken off your engagement to Dex. Are you mental? He's well fit.'

'It's just that my feelings towards him aren't the same anymore,' replies Tina.

'So why are you still wearing his ring?'

'Oh, my feelings towards the ring haven't changed a bit!'

---

Two Essex Girls are discussing where to go to eat. One says: 'I fancy that new place in the High Street that serves all-day breakfast.'

'Oh, I dunno,' says the other. 'I could never eat that much breakfast.'

---

Kelly and Shelley are building a wooden house. Kelly picks up a nail, hammers it in, then picks up another nail and throws it away. She repeats the process over and over again. After this has been going on for some time, Shelley asks: 'Why do you keep throwing half the nails away?'

'Bee-ayve!' says Kelly. 'Those nails are pointed at the wrong end.'

'How could you be so stupid?' says Shelley. 'They're for the other side of the house!'

An Essex Girl is booking a holiday for her and her mates and is tasked with sorting out their travel plans, so she phones British Airways. 'Excuse me,' she says. 'How long does it take to fly from Heathrow to San Francisco?'

'Just a minute,' says the operator.

'That's quick,' says the Essex Girl. And she hangs up.

Two teenage school netball teams – one from Suffolk, the other from Essex – are travelling by double-decker bus for a tournament in London. The Suffolk Girls sit on the lower deck while the Essex Girls are all upstairs. The Suffolk Girls are having a great time, laughing and singing, until one of them realises that it is totally silent upstairs where the Essex Girls are sitting. So she goes upstairs to investigate and finds all the Essex Girls rigid with fear, staring straight ahead at the road, and gripping the seats in front of them with white knuckles.

'What's the matter?' asks the Suffolk Girl. 'We're having a great time downstairs.'

'It's all right for you,' says one of the Essex Girls. 'You've got a driver.'

Two Essex Girls are away on an adventure weekend in the Lake District. The archery and rifle activities pass off without incident but during the orienteering exercise the pair become hopelessly lost. They are unable to get a signal on their mobile phones and all their cries for help prove in vain. So they sit down forlornly and discuss what to do next.

Then, eyeing the weaponry, one says: 'Didn't the guide suggest that we should shoot into the air to summon help if we got lost?'

'You're right,' says the other Essex Girl, and she grabs the bag containing the weapons.

But after another three hours and a dozen shots, still no one comes to their rescue.

'Do you think anyone will ever find us?' asks the first Essex Girl dejectedly.

'I hope so,' says the other. 'We've only got two arrows left.'

*Did you hear about the Essex Girl who visited New York and arranged to meet her friend at the corner of Walk and Don't Walk?*

Maxine and Shelley are walking down Brentwood High Street. ''Ere, Shell,' says Maxine, 'look at that dog with no eyes.'

Shelley says: 'How am I supposed to see it?'

Pat drains all the water from her swimming pool.

'Why did you do that?' asks her pal Janine.

Pat explains: 'I want to practise diving but I can't swim.'

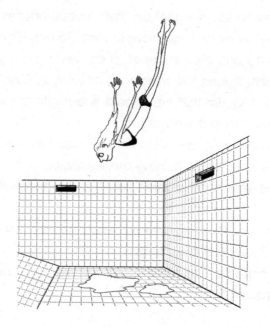

Nicola and Debbie go into a café and order two drinks. They then take their tuna salad sandwiches from their lunch boxes and start to eat. Seeing this, the waiter tells them: 'Sorry, but you can't eat your own sandwiches in here.'

Nicola and Debbie look at each other, shrug their shoulders and exchange sandwiches.

Stacey and Mandy are walking along Southend Beach one summer's night. After a while Stacey turns to her friend and says: 'Mand, which do you think is nearer, the moon or Australia?'

'Helloooo!' says Mandy. 'Can you see Australia?'

---

Sharon and Tracey are walking through the woods when Sharon glances down and says: 'Oh, look at the deer tracks.'

Tracey says: 'Those aren't deer tracks. They're fox tracks.'

'Bee-ayve!' says Sharon. 'I'm telling you, they're deer tracks!'

'You should've gone to Specsavers,' mocks Tracey. 'They're fox tracks.'

They keep arguing until fifteen minutes later they are hit by a train.

---

Two Essex Girls are driving along a road by a wheat field when they spot another Essex Girl in the middle of the field rowing a boat. The driver turns to her friend and says: 'It's Essex Girls like that who gave us all a bad name.'

'I know,' says her friend, 'and if I could swim, I'd go out there and drown her.'

Cara is sitting on the train opposite a man reading a newspaper. The headline reads: 'Five Brazilian soldiers killed.'

'That's terrible,' says Cara, turning to her friend. 'How many is a Brazilian?'

Sharon says to Kelly: 'I had a terrible time last night. I had to slap my boyfriend three times.'

'What,' says Kelly, 'to keep him in line?'

'No,' says Sharon, 'to keep him awake.'

---

A Surrey Girl, a Kent Girl and an Essex Girl go on holiday to Ayia Napa. The Surrey Girl takes three bottles of factor 30 sun cream, the Kent Girl takes a sun umbrella, and the Essex Girl takes a car door.

The other two ask the Essex Girl: 'Why have you brought a car door?'

She explains: 'If it gets too hot, we can roll the window down.'

---

Kelly says to Sam: 'I'm leaving Romford next year.'

'Why?' asks Sam.

'I'm going to some place called Jeopardy. I'm not sure where in England it is, but I heard on the news that there're thousands of jobs there.'

Billie, Davina and Wendy enter a pub's weekly prize draw. Billie wins first prize (a set of hair straighteners), Davina wins second prize (a twenty-minute sunbed session), and Wendy wins third prize (a toilet brush).

When they meet up again in the pub the following week, they discuss their prizes.

'What do you think of my hair?' asks Billie. 'The straighteners are wicked.'

'The sunbed session was great, too,' says Davina. 'How's your toilet brush, Wend?'

'Not so good,' sighs Wendy. 'I think I'll go back to using paper.'

Julie and a dozen of her friends are out celebrating her birthday in a Chelmsford nightclub. They've been knocking back the Bacardi Breezers for a couple of hours and are well oiled by the time she's chatted up at the bar by a handsome stranger.

He says to her: 'Happy birthday. Listen, if I can guess how old you are, can I have a snog?'

'OK, you're on,' she laughs, 'but I'm telling you, there's no way you'll guess how old I am.'

'Twenty-five,' he says confidently.

'I don't bloody believe it!' she exclaims. 'How did you guess that?'

'I'm psychic,' he replies. 'Plus, it says it on your badge.'

A row broke out among the Essex Schools' Synchronised Swimming team when Denise accused Paige of copying her.

Tracey comes to a river and sees her friend Chantelle on the opposite bank. 'Yoo-hoo!' shouts Tracey. 'How can I get to the other side?'

Chantelle looks at her blankly and shouts back: 'You *are* on the other side!'

An Essex Girl and a Surrey Girl go into a café and order two lattes. After a few minutes, the Essex Girl complains: 'Why does my eye hurt every time I take a sip of coffee?'

The Surrey Girl suggests: 'Try taking the spoon out.'

# CARS AND MOTORS

An Essex Girl is out with her boyfriend when his car breaks down.

He asks her to check that the hazard warning lights are working, so she gets out and walks to the back of the car to take a look.

'Are they on?' he calls out.

'Yes, no, yes, no, yes, no, yes . . .'

Two Essex Girls are struggling to unlock the door of their Mercedes with a coat hanger.

When the girl with the hanger pauses for breath, her friend says: 'Hurry up! It's starting to rain and the top is down!'

*How do you get rid of an Essex Girl?*
Tell her your car's being repaired.

*How is an Essex Girl like a moped?*
A lot of people ride her, but nobody admits it.

---

An Essex Girl is involved in a nasty car crash that has left her trapped and bleeding. The paramedics soon arrive at the accident site and hurry to her aid . . .

Medic: It's OK, I'm a paramedic and I'm going to ask you some questions.
Girl: OK.
Medic: What's your name?
Girl: Sharon.
Medic: OK, Sharon, is this your car?
Sharon: Yes.
Medic: Can you move your legs?
Sharon: Yes.
Medic: Where are you bleeding from?
Sharon: Romford, mate.

---

*Why was the Essex Girl disappointed when she got her driving licence?*
Because she got an F in sex.

Dave is driving along the A12 with his pit bull terrier in the back seat. The dog is barking continuously.

Eventually, the noise alerts a police patrol, who order Dave to pull over.

The officer steps out of the car, eyes the vicious-looking dog and says to Dave: 'Excuse me, sir, but does that dog have a licence?'

'It's all right, Officer,' says Dave, 'he don't need one. You see, I do all the driving.'

*Why do Essex Girls prefer cars with*
*sunroofs?*
There's more leg room.

An ambulance arrives at the scene of a car crash on the A127 near Basildon. The paramedic goes over to the dazed girl passenger and asks: 'How many fingers have I got up?'

'Oh my God!' she squeals. 'I'm paralysed from the waist down!'

Kelly and Tracey are filling their cars at a Billericay petrol station. Kelly says: 'The price of petrol these days is doin' my 'ead in!'

Tracey says: 'It doesn't really affect me. I always just put in £10 worth.'

An Essex Girl is speeding down the A12 in her BMW convertible when she is pulled over by an Essex policewoman. The Essex cop asks to see the Essex Girl's driving licence.

The Essex Girl rummages through her Louis Vuitton bag, but can't find the licence anywhere. 'What does it look like?' she asks, sounding increasingly agitated.

The policewoman replies: 'It's square and has your picture on it.'

Eventually the Essex Girl finds a square mirror in her bag, looks at it and hands it to the policewoman, saying, 'Here it is, Officer.'

The Essex policewoman looks at the mirror, hands it back to the Essex Girl and says: 'It's OK, you can go. I didn't realise you were a cop.'


*How is an Essex Girl like a halogen headlamp?*
They both get screwed on the front of a Ford Fiesta.


Kev and his new girlfriend go for a drive in Constable Country. Starting to feel randy, they find a quiet spot and start to have sex in the back seat. However, she is a tall girl and the car is a bit cramped, so they decide to carry on underneath the vehicle where there is more leg room.

A few minutes later, a police officer happens to

be passing and announces that he is arresting the couple for indecent exposure.

'You're 'aving a laugh!' says Kev. 'I'm not doing anything wrong. I'm just fixing my car.'

'You're having sex,' replies the officer icily. 'And I know that to be a fact for three reasons. Firstly, you have no car tools out. Secondly, I can see a second pair of legs in addition to yours. And thirdly, your car's been stolen!'

*An Essex Girl read that most car accidents happen within twenty miles of the home, so she moved to Kent.*

An Essex Boy takes his Ford Fiesta to the garage in the hope that the service manager can cure the strange noise the car keeps making when cornering. The job is passed on to a mechanic with a repair order that reads: 'Check for clunking sound when going around corners.'

The mechanic takes the car on a test drive and, sure enough, whenever he turns a corner there is a clunking sound. Eventually he traces the cause of the problem and returns the repair order to the service manager with a note that reads: 'Removed bowling ball from boot.'

*How can you tell if an Essex Girl has been sitting in your car?*
The gearstick is wet.

*What's the difference between an Essex Girl and a Ferrari?*
You don't lend the Ferrari out to your friends.

After buying a Christmas tree, an Essex Girl finds that it is too big to fit in her car.

'You'll have to cut the top off,' says the shop-keeper.

'That's a good idea,' says the Essex Girl. 'I've always wanted a convertible.'

*Why are car maintenance classes in Essex schools only able to use the car on Mondays, Wednesdays and Fridays?*
Because on Tuesdays and Thursdays the sex education class uses it.

Shelley runs into Billericay police station. 'Someone's just stolen my car,' she wails. 'I was parked outside the nail bar, and when I came out, I saw my car being driven away! OMG! What am I going to do?'

'Just try and stay calm,' says the desk sergeant. 'I'm sure everything will be fine. Now did you get a description of the thief?'

'No,' says Shelley, reaching into her bag for a piece of paper, 'but I did get the registration number.'

An Essex Girl calls over a passing policeman to report that thieves have been in her car.

'The little toerags!' she says. 'They've stolen the dashboard, the steering wheel, the brake pedal, even the accelerator.'

'Miss,' explains the policeman patiently, 'you're in the back seat.'

An Essex Girl is driving along the road when she is stopped by a police patrol car. An officer gets out and asks her to identify herself. She pulls a small mirror from her handbag, looks in it and says: 'Yes, Officer, it's definitely me.'

*What's the worst thing about having sex with
an Essex Girl?*
Bucket seats.

A policeman pulls over an Essex Girl after she has been driving the wrong way along a one-way street. He asks her: 'Do you know where you were going?'

'No,' she replies, 'but wherever it is it must be bad cos all the people were leaving.'

An Essex Girl is driving home one night when she is pulled over by traffic cops. The officer steps out of his car and tells her: 'You've been driving erratically. I'm going to have to give you a breathalyser test to determine whether you're under the influence of alcohol.'

So she breathes into the bag and he studies the result. 'Hmmm,' he says, 'it looks like you've had a couple of stiff ones.'

The Essex Girl blushes and squeals: 'Shuuut uuup! You're not telling me it shows that too?'

A motorist stops at a country ford and asks an Essex Girl standing by the side of the lane how deep the water is.

'Just a couple of inches,' she replies.

So the motorist drives into the ford and his car promptly disappears beneath the surface in a cauldron of bubbles.

'That's odd,' thinks the Essex Girl. 'The water only goes halfway up on those ducks.'

An Essex Girl is stopped by a police officer who asks to see her licence. 'I don't believe it!' she squeals. 'I wish you policemen would get your act together. Yesterday you take my licence away, and today you expect me to show it to you!'

An Essex Girl is driving down a country lane north of Colchester when she starts swerving the car, first to the right, then to the left. This goes on for several miles until she is stopped by a passing police car.

An officer gets out and asks her: 'Why are you driving so unsteadily? You've been swerving all over the road. You could have caused a serious accident.'

'You're not gonna believe this,' says the Essex Girl breathlessly, 'but I'm being stalked by trees. They're following me everywhere. I was driving along without a care in the world, thinking I must get my nails done tomorrow, but then when I looked up there was a tree right in front of me. So I swerved to the left but there was another tree. So I swerved to the right and there was another tree. And it went on and on like that. I tell you, it was doin' my 'ead in!'

Calmly the officer reaches through the side window to the rear-view mirror and says: 'Miss, there were no trees. It was your air freshener.'

An Essex Girl is driving to Lakeside. After an hour on the road, she sees a sign which says 'Lakeside Left'. So she turns around despondently and goes home.

---

A policeman stops an Essex Girl for speeding. 'You were doing 60mph in a 30mph zone. What do you think you were playing at?'

'I'm sorry, Officer,' smiles the Essex Girl sweetly, 'but you see my brakes failed about two miles back and I was hurrying to get home before I caused an accident.'

---

Having just passed her driving test, a seventeen-year-old girl went to a used-car showroom in Rayleigh to buy a second-hand Ford Ka. She saw one she liked but before driving it away she had a few questions for the salesman.

'You'll have to excuse me,' she said, 'but this is my first car and I don't know a lot about cars. So how do the windscreen wipers work?'

The salesman showed her the button to operate the wipers.

'Thank you,' she said, 'and where does the oil go?'

The salesman lifted up the bonnet and showed her where the oil went.

'Oh, you're amazing!' she said. 'How do you know all this stuff? I'm sure I'll never remember it. Things go in one ear and out the other with me. Brain like a sieve, my mum always says.'

'I'm sure you're not that bad,' said the salesman. 'You'll soon pick it up.'

'I hope so,' she laughed. 'Oh, one more thing: petrol. I know that's very important.'

'Yes, the petrol cap is round here,' he said. 'In town traffic this car should do about forty-five miles to the gallon. Make sure you never run out of petrol.'

'Oh, right,' she said, taking in his advice. 'Why, will it hurt the car if I drive it when there's no petrol in it?'

For once a salesman was lost for words.

---

When an Essex Girl gets caught speeding, a police officer pulls her over and asks to see her licence. As she searches for it, he craftily unzips his trousers.

As she looks up, she sighs: 'Oh no, not another breathalyser!'

---

*Why did the Essex Girl drive her car into church?*

Because Dave's Motors said she needed to take it in for a service.

Paige is driving home in her BMW when she gets caught in a terrible hailstorm which leaves a series of dents in the bodywork of her car. So she takes it to a garage where the mechanic decides to have a joke at her expense. He tells her: 'When you get home, all you have to do is blow into the exhaust as hard as you can and all the dents will pop out.' When she gets home, she follows the mechanic's instructions, huffing and puffing into the exhaust pipe for all she is worth. But after twenty minutes of this, she is dismayed to see that the dents remain. 'What's occurring?' asks her flatmate Tracey, alerted by the noise. Paige tells her what the mechanic had ordered her to do.

'Are you ever stupid?' says Tracey. 'Duh! Don't you know you have to wind up the windows first?'

*Why do Essex girls like tilt steering?*
More headroom.

An Essex Girl is trying to sell her old VW but is struggling to attract a buyer because the car has over 200,000 miles on the clock. One day she is pouring out her problems to a Surrey Girl at work when the Surrey Girl whispers: 'There is a way of making the car easier to sell, but it's not legal.'

'I don't care whether or not it's legal,' says the Essex Girl. 'I just want to sell my bloody car.'

'OK,' says the Surrey Girl. 'Here is the address of a friend of mine who owns a car repair shop. Tell him I sent you and he'll sort it out. After that, you shouldn't have any difficulty selling your car.'

The next day, the Essex Girl goes to see the mechanic. A few weeks later, she bumps into the Surrey Girl at work.

'Did you manage to sell your car?' asks the Surrey Girl.

'No,' replies the Essex Girl. 'Why should I? It only has 30,000 miles on the clock!'

*Why do Essex Girls drive VWs?*
Because they can't spell Porsche.

---

After stopping at a petrol station, Sharon has just paid at the cash desk when she realises she has locked her keys in the car. So she asks the attendant for a coat hanger in the hope of using it to open the car door. The attendant gives her a hanger and she takes it outside.

Ten minutes later, he goes out to her car to see how she is doing. He finds her crouched down by the door, carefully manoeuvring the hanger through a crack in the driver's side window, while her friend Tracey in the passenger seat says: 'A bit more to the left, down a little, a bit more to the right . . .'

*Did you hear about the Essex Girl who sold
her car to get some petrol money?*

*Why did the Essex Girl fail her driving test?*
Every time the car stopped, she jumped in
the back seat.

*What does an Essex Girl call safe sex?*
A padded dashboard.

---

A lorry is driving along the A12 when an Essex Girl pulls her car alongside and shouts: 'Driver, you're losing your load!'

'Get lost!' yells the lorry driver.

Two miles further down the road, the Essex Girl again draws alongside the lorry and yells across to the driver: 'You're definitely losing your load!'

'Do one!' exclaims the lorry driver impatiently.

A mile further on, the Essex Girl pulls alongside the lorry once more and shouts: 'I'm not joking, driver. You really are losing your load!'

'For the last time, go to hell!' yells the lorry driver. 'I'm gritting!'

---

*What's the first thing an Essex Girl learns
when she has driving lessons?*
You can sit upright in a car.

*Why did the Essex Girl bury her driving licence?*
Because it had expired.

---

An Essex Girl is driving along the A13 when her mobile rings. It's her boyfriend, Mick, and he warns her: 'Treacle, I just heard on the news that there's a car going the wrong way on the A13. Be careful.'

'It's not just one car!' she squeals. 'There's hundreds of them!'

---

# WORKING
## NINE
## TO FIVE

On her second day in a new job, an Essex Girl is standing next to an office fax machine crying her eyes out.

'What's wrong?' asks a sympathetic male colleague.

'It's this damn machine!' she wails. 'I can't get it to send a fax.'

Patiently he shows her how to do it and the sheet of paper is sent through successfully.

'There!' he says. 'It's quite straightforward really.'

But when she lifts the lid and sees the piece of paper, she starts crying again. 'It hasn't worked at all! It's still there!'

An Essex Girl goes for a job interview at TK Maxx. The woman conducting the interview says: 'I see from your application form that under "previous employment" you have put "babysitter". Would you mind telling me what your reason for leaving was?'

'Yeah,' replies the Essex Girl. 'They came home unexpectedly.'

*Why was the Essex Girl talking into an envelope?*
She was sending a voicemail.

To earn some money during the school holidays, Debbie took a part-time job working in the kitchen of a Chelmsford restaurant. The restaurant was part of a chain, so Debbie didn't think the work would be too demanding, but she had reckoned without the head chef, a man who clearly modelled himself on Gordon Ramsay. He had already got through three kitchen assistants in the previous month and frequently reduced his staff to tears. The restaurant manager who hired Debbie had warned her that the chef could be a little 'temperamental' but she needed the job.

Her first evening at work was a busy Friday. The place was packed and the chef was getting flustered, his face reddening by the minute. As she had no experience of working in a restaurant, Debbie was given basic tasks like dishwashing, surface cleaning and keeping an eye on slow-cooking dishes. He had already bawled her out twice over minor mistakes when he flew into yet another rage.

'Were you born stupid?' he bellowed. 'Or have you had to work at it? I thought I told you to notice when the soup boiled over!'

'I did,' protested Debbie. 'It was half past eight.'

---

The boss asks his Essex Girl PA why she is late for work. 'You're not gonna believe this!' she trills. 'On my way in I saw this terrible road accident. It was simply awful. The driver looked to have broken both legs, his passenger had horrific head injuries, and there was blood all over the road. Thank God I took that first-aid course last year. All my training came back to me in a flash.'

'What did you do?' asks the boss.

She says: 'I sat down and put my head between my knees to stop myself from fainting.'

---

*How can you tell when an Essex Girl has sent a fax?*
There's a stamp on it.

An executive is interviewing an Essex Girl for a job. In an attempt to discover something about her personality, he asks her: 'If you could have a conversation with someone, living or dead, who would it be?'

The Essex Girl gives the question careful consideration before answering firmly: 'The living one. Definitely.'

*An Essex Girl who worked as a secretary
always filed her nails – under N.*

Joanne from Ilford was working for a multi-national company in the heart of London. One day she had to attend a fire safety demonstration along with about twenty other members of staff in the car park at head office.

The company's fire safety official lit a small fire in a bucket and then issued instructions on how to operate the extinguisher. He told the assembled staff: 'Pull the pin like a hand grenade, and then depress the trigger to release the foam.'

Joanne hid at the back, hoping to avoid his eye, but to her horror, she was chosen to demonstrate the procedure. He handed her the extinguisher, but in her nervousness, she forgot to pull the pin.

Offering a helpful hint, he said: 'Like a hand grenade, remember?'

So she pulled the pin and hurled the extinguisher at the fire.

An Essex Girl is filling out an application form. At the bottom where it says 'Sign here', she writes down 'Pisces'.

On her first day at work in an office, Mandy is asked to go out and fetch the morning coffees. Eager to impress, she grabs a large thermos and hurries to the nearest Starbucks. Holding up the thermos, she asks the guy at the counter: 'Is this big enough to hold six cups of coffee?'

'Yes, I should think so,' he replies.

'Oh, good,' says Mandy, relieved. 'In that case, give me two lattes, two black and two cappuccinos.'

*Why did the Essex Girl nurse tiptoe past the medicine cabinet?*
She didn't want to wake the sleeping pills.

An Essex Girl working in a Brentwood nail bar is in floods of tears. 'OMG!' she tells her boss. 'I've just received a text to say that my mother's dead.'

'That's terrible news,' says her boss sympathetically. 'Why don't you take the rest of the day off?'

'No, it's OK,' says the Essex Girl between sobs. 'Being surrounded by people and helping to enrich their lives by giving them perfectly manicured nails helps to take my mind off my personal tragedy.'

Even so, the boss keeps a close eye on her for

signs of distress and, sure enough, an hour later the Essex Girl is crying her heart out again.

'What's happened?' asks her boss.

'You're not gonna believe this!' wails the Essex Girl. 'But I've had a text from my sister and her mum's died too!'

---

Staying at a posh West End hotel for a work conference, an Essex Girl phones reception in a blind panic. 'Help! I'm trapped in my room,' she wails. 'I can't get out.'

'What's the problem?' asks the receptionist. 'Have you tried the door?'

'But there are only three doors in here,' says the Essex Girl. 'One is the bathroom, one is the closet, and the other one has a sign on it that says, "Do Not Disturb".'

---

Sharon turns up for work one day wearing only one glove.

'Why have you only got one glove on?' asks her boss.

'Well,' explains Sharon, 'I was watching the weather forecast on TV last night, and it said that it was going to be nice and sunny today but on the other hand it could be quite cold.'

*What do you do when an Essex Girl soldier throws a pin at you?*
Run like hell because she's got a grenade in her mouth.

Chantelle arrives home from her first day of commuting from Chelmsford to Liverpool Street. Her mother notices that she is looking tired and asks whether she is OK.

'Not really,' says Chantelle. 'I'm feeling nauseous from sitting backwards on the train for half an hour.'

'You poor thing,' says her mother sympathetically. 'Why didn't you ask the person sitting opposite you to switch seats?'

'I couldn't,' says Chantelle. 'There wasn't anyone in the seat opposite me.'

*What happened to the Essex Girl tap dancer?*
She slipped off and fell in the sink.

An Essex Girl goes for a job interview at Lakeside.

'How old are you?' asks the interviewer.

The Essex Girl starts counting on her fingers. 'Uh, let me see now, twenty-four.'

'And what is your height?'

The Essex Girl gets out a tape measure and measures herself from head to toe. 'Uh, five foot three.'

Sensing that this is going to be a struggle, the interviewer decides to slip her an easier question. 'What is your name?'

The Essex Girl mouths something to herself for a few moments before replying: 'Stacey.'

'What were you saying to yourself just then?' asks the interviewer.

'Oh, I was trying to remember that song: "Happy birthday to you, happy birthday to you, happy birthday dear . . ."'

*Why did the Essex Girl chef roast a chicken for two and a half days?*
The instructions said 'cook for half an hour per pound', and she weighed 120.

An Essex Girl is working in the post room of an office. She goes to collect the mail from where it lies by the front door, but immediately starts wailing.

'What's the matter?' asks her concerned colleague.

The Essex Girl cries: 'There's a letter for me marked: "Do Not Bend".'

'So? What's the problem?'

'Well, how am I supposed to pick it up?'

*What's black and fuzzy and hangs from the ceiling?*
An Essex Girl electrician.

Mandy, Tracey and Kelly are training to become police detectives. To test their skills in recognising a suspect, the police sergeant shows each girl in turn a photo for five seconds. 'This is your suspect,' he tells Mandy. 'How would you recognise him?'

'Easy peasy lemon squeezy,' replies Mandy. 'I'll soon catch him cos he only has one eye.'

The sergeant looks at her in disbelief. 'Er, that's because the photo is showing his profile.'

Hoping for a more sensible answer, he then flashes the photo to Tracey and says: 'This is your suspect. How would you recognise him?'

'You're 'aving a laugh, ain't yer?' giggles Tracey. 'He'd be soooo easy to catch cos he only has one ear.'

The sergeant buries his head in his hands in despair. 'What's wrong with you two? Of course only one eye and one ear are showing because it's a photo of his profile! Is that the best answer you can come up with?'

Fearing another stupid reply, he then shows the picture to Kelly for five seconds and snaps: 'This is your suspect. How would you recognise him? And think hard before opening your mouth.'

Kelly considers the photo carefully and states: 'The suspect wears contact lenses.'

The sergeant is just relieved to hear a sensible answer even though he has no idea whether Kelly's theory is true or not. He tells her: 'That's certainly an interesting suggestion. Wait here a minute while I check his file to find out if he does actually wear contact lenses.'

After checking the suspect's file on the computer, the sergeant returns with a broad smile on his face. 'Great work!' he tells Kelly. 'The suspect does wear contact lenses. You've clearly got what it takes to become a detective. Tell me, how were you able to make such an astute observation?'

'It was obvious,' says Kelly. 'He can't wear glasses because he only has one eye and one ear.'

As part of a work aptitude test, an Essex Girl is asked to spell Mississippi. 'Which?' she says. 'The river or the state?'

An Essex Girl gets a job as a keeper at London Zoo, but on her second morning she is summoned to a meeting with the head keeper.

'You stupid girl!' he yells. 'You left the door to the lions' cage open all night.'

'Take a chill pill,' she replies. 'What's all the fuss about? Who's going to steal a lion?'

Two men meet in the corridor at work. 'Did you hear what happened?' asks one.

'No,' says the other.

'The MD died this morning.'

'My God! How?'

'He was working through lunch when he had a heart attack. Nobody was around except his PA – you know, the one from Basildon with the orange skin and pneumatic boobs.'

'Yes, I know the one. Some of the guys think she's hot.'

'Maybe, but she's a few sandwiches short of a picnic.'

'What makes you say that?'

'Apparently the MD kept screaming at her to call 999, but she just stood there waiting for him to give her the rest of the phone number.'

A Surrey Girl, a Kent Girl and an Essex Girl work together in a Westminster office. Each day their female boss leaves work early, so finally the three decide to do the same. The Surrey Girl is thrilled to leave early so she can get home to play with her baby son. The Kent Girl is thrilled to leave early so she can go to the gym. And the Essex Girl is thrilled to leave early so she can get home and surprise her husband. But when she gets home, she hears muffled noises coming from her bedroom. Slowly she opens the door and is horrified to see her husband in bed with her boss. Gently she closes the door and creeps back out of the house.

The next day at coffee break, the Surrey Girl and

the Kent Girl reveal they are planning to leave early again and ask the Essex Girl if she is going to do the same.

'No way!' says the Essex Girl. 'I almost got caught yesterday.'

Julie and Abi worked together in a Chelmsford office.

As befits young women, their lunchtime conversations frequently focused on their respective love lives and old boyfriends. One day Julie asked Abi: 'What's the best sex you've ever had?'

'Oh, definitely with a guy I went out with last year. Matt, his name was. He was so imaginative.'

'Like how?' pressed Julie.

'Well, I remember once he sat me on top of the washing machine when it was on fast spin and made me take all my clothes off.'

'Never!' said Julie excitedly. 'That must have been an amazing sensation.'

'Yeah, it was,' said Abi. 'It sent these vibrations through my whole body. I just had one roaring orgasm after another and that was before he even entered me. Mind you, I'll never be able to use that launderette again.'

Chantelle is in trouble for always being late in for work. Eventually she is summoned by HR to a disciplinary hearing to explain herself.

'The thing is,' she says, 'I get up in the morning, I shower, I look in the mirror. Then I do my hair. But sometimes it takes so long that I miss my train. I'm sorry, I really will try harder.'

Hearing this, her boss has a cunning plan. He asks one of Chantelle's friends in the office to sneak into her bathroom and remove the mirror from the wall without her knowing. The friend duly removes the mirror, but Chantelle's timekeeping does not improve. In fact, it gets worse and when she fails to show up for work for three days in a row she is ordered to face another disciplinary hearing.

Asked why she was absent for three days, Chantelle explains: 'I get up in the morning, I shower, I look in the mirror. But I couldn't see Chantelle, so I thought Chantelle must have already left for work.'

*Why did the Essex Girl secretary chop off her fingers?*
So she could write short hand.

Needing some money to buy spray tan and new hair extensions, an Essex Girl offers to help a farmer plough his field.

'I don't know,' says the farmer. 'Ploughing requires a steady hand, and I'm not sure a young girl like you is up to the task.'

'That's bang out of order!' says the Essex Girl. 'That's sexist, ageist and probably racist, that is. I've a good mind to report you.'

'OK, OK,' says the farmer, backing down. 'I'll give you a chance. Take the plough and I'll watch you. But you'll have to take off your white stilettos first.'

So the Essex Girl puts on more suitable footwear and begins ploughing. Unsurprisingly, her lines are all over the place. 'I don't get it,' she wails. 'I'm watching the plough to make sure I don't go crooked.'

'That's where you're going wrong,' says the farmer. 'Don't look at the plough. Instead watch where you're going. Look at the far end of the field, pick out an object and head straight for it. That way, you'll cut a straight row every time.'

Having given his advice, the farmer returns to the house to attend to some paperwork, leaving the Essex Girl to plough the field unsupervised. When he returns, the farmer sees to his horror that she has cut the worst row ever. Her lines run all over the field in crazy circles.

'What the hell happened?' he yells. 'I've never seen such a terrible field. There's not one straight line!'

'But I did what you said,' she protests. 'I fixed my sights on that dog playing at the far end of the field.'

*Why are Essex Girls only allowed half-hour lunch breaks?*
Because if they took an hour, you'd have to retrain them.

Three pregnant work colleagues (an Essex Girl, a Surrey Girl and a Sussex Girl) meet up in a café and start talking about their pregnancies.

The Surrey Girl declares: 'I'm going to have a boy.'

'How do you know?' asks the Essex Girl.

'Because,' explains the Surrey Girl, 'I was underneath when we did it and so it's going to be a boy.'

The Sussex Girl says: 'In that case, my baby is a girl because I was on top.'

The Essex Girl then starts bawling: 'I'm going to have a puppy.'

An Essex Girl gets a job as a teacher. One day she notices a boy standing alone in the school field while all the other kids are running around having fun. She takes pity on him and decides to speak to him.

'Are you OK?' she asks.

'Yes,' he replies.

'You can go and play with the other kids, you know,' she says.

'It's best I stay here.'

'Why?'

'Because,' says the boy, 'I'm the f**king goalkeeper!'

If you enjoyed *The Essex Joke Book*, you might also be tickled by the books in our bestselling *Man Walks into a Bar* series...

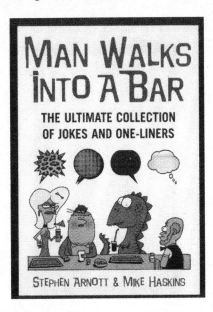

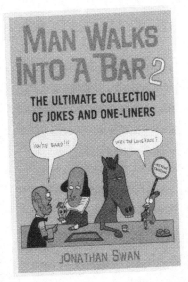

'Completely and utterly hilarious' Stephen Fry

Ever been screwed over by predictive text on your smart phone? You are not alone. *Damn You, Autocorrect!* brings together the most outrageously funny and painfully embarrassing posts from the hit website damnyouautocorrect.com, presenting hundreds of hilarious cases of autocorrect sabotaging your messages – and your life. Read this book before you hit send.

*To find out more about our latest publications,*
*sign up to our newsletter at:*
*www.eburypublishing.co.uk*